A
Substitute Teacher's
Guide to Survival

15063-MEHR

A

Substitute Teacher's Guide to Survival

Judy Saul Mehr

15063-MEHR

To order additional copies of this book, contact:
Xlibris Corporation
1-888-795-4274
www.Xlibris.com
Orders@Xlibris.com

Contents

15063-MEHR

I DEDICATE THIS BOOK TO MY CHILDREN,
JOEL AND DENISE, WHO GAVE ME SO MUCH SUPPORT
DURING THE PROCESS OF WRITING THIS WORK.
I WOULD ALSO LIKE TO THANK MY MANY FRIENDS
AND MY FAVORITE COUSIN, SIDNEY SHERES,
FOR HELPING ME WITH THE EDITING.
AND LAST, BUT NOT LEAST, I DEDICATE THIS BOOK
TO ALL THOSE BRAVE SUBSTITUTE TEACHERS
WHO ARE INSTRUMENTAL IN KEEPING ORDER
IN THE CLASSROOMS WHEN CHAOS IS A PROBABILITY.

INTRODUCTION

Dear Substitutes and Sympathetic Fellow Humans,

Substitute Teachers of America, you are ESSENTIALS. Therefore, I urge you to be proud of what you do. The show cannot go on without you, which is why I want you to think of yourselves not only as stand-in performers, but the lifeline of schools. No matter how small the role, the show must have an understudy or the performance may be canceled.

Substitute teachers are the unsung heroes of all schools, beginning from kindergarten and extending through the twelfth grade. My objective in writing this book is to extol the virtues of substitute teachers, and warn the would-be-subs of the perils they will encounter. In doing this, I will try to inject a little humor into a job that too often is not very amusing. Then again, how many jobs are? I myself tend to find humor in almost any situation, which is why Erma Bombeck, who could find humor even in the face of adversity, has always been my hero and my inspiration. I have therefore decided to share some insights and perhaps a little wisdom of what honestly has not always been an easy task. Furthermore, I know this information can be beneficial to new teachers or student teachers that are just embarking on a career in education. This book is also meant to support and enhance the image of subs so they will not be stereotyped as the archetypical school fool, but instead be valued as a school tool.

I hope this book will also enlighten parents on the behavior of many of their "adorable" children in a classroom situation because, dear parents, your children can be so totally different when they are amongst their peers. I am sure, after reading this book, that many of you parents will be in denial and will not believe your precious child can exhibit such inappropriate behavior.

Whenever I told people I was a sub, I would get one of two reactions. Either they would say, "That must be a horrible job," which really made me feel great, or they would smile or say "I remember my experiences with subs." By their sinister look, I knew what they were thinking, and I'm not either psychic or paranoid.

Almost everyone has a "sub story." Jack Webb on the "Dragnet" series always ended an episode by remarking that there were eight million people in New York City, and each one had his own story. And so it goes with substitutes. Either you have been one and have your own anecdotes, or you have had one and remember funny experiences. In either case, everyone knows that subs are a prime target for practical jokes. Some of these "cute" pranks may include locking the sub out of the room, turning slides upside-down in a slide projector carousel, switching videos in the VCR, or messing up a movie projector so that when it is turned on it's on full blast. Aren't kids adorable? Actually most of them *are*, until they come across a sub they're not acquainted with. Then many of them become great masters in the art of using aliases when they misbehave.

Whenever I caught a child throwing something across the room or deliberately dropping his books to scare the heck out of me (it usually worked), I would ask him his name and often the name he gave me was not his own. How did I know he was using an alias? The class would start giggling, a telltale sign, or the child whose name the culprit was using would pipe up and tell the truth because he didn't want to get in trouble.

Substitute teaching is truly an adventure beginning with your first day at school in a perhaps less than friendly office environment, to having to teach without lesson plans. You need to be a great ad libber in order to be an effective sub.

Although most of my own subbing experience took place at the high school level, I was once a full time elementary school music teacher and also substituted at that level. Thus, I am enlightened on the behavior of children of all ages and how they operate. Youngsters can adeptly perform major surgery on subs who are idealistic and inexperienced. It seems to be an innate skill most children possess. (Am I sounding cynical to you so far? I'm sure I am.)

As in most professions, you don't really "know" what is in store for you until you actually work at the job. I believe it is especially true in the teaching profession because you are constantly dealing with a wide variety of personalities and situations, and therefore no two days are ever alike in a classroom. So in essence, this book is not really a "how to" book, but rather, it is more of a "what to expect" book.

Since the inception of this book, I have found the National Substitute Teachers Alliance *http://www.nstasubs.org/)* and an NEA study of the plight of subs, (http://www.nea.org/teaching/substudy.html) and two articles, which have appeared in separate newspapers concerning substitute teachers. One article in the Washington Post addressed the possible elimination of substitutes in the D.C. school system, and the other, a local Montgomery County, Maryland paper, acknowledged, what I've known all along, that subs are "getting no respect." (I said it first. Well, maybe second or third!) In any case, both articles were in agreement, substantiating the fact that subs are valuable assets to schools and essentially little or no training is provided concerning discipline, health and safety, weapons, drugs or children with special needs. Although some subs may have had classroom experience, many have had little or no exposure to a classroom full of eager youngsters ready to try to outwit unsuspecting substitutes. Therefore, I propose a period of orientation, including uniformity in school policies, be rendered to every substitute teacher. In other words, subs need much more nurturing, support and training than has been afforded them in the past. They need a certain amount of warning as well!

As you all know, substitutes are affectionately referred to as "The Sub", which might have the connotation of one who is a SUBordinate instructor. We hope that is not true. But the term "sub" has an ambiguous meaning. Are they are referring to you as a SUBmarine?—Nah. Is there something SUBversive about you? I doubt it. Could they be talking about a hero (SUB) sandwich? I doubt that too, although anyone who substitutes in a school should receive a medal for heroism since the job often entails going into combat. We all know however, "sub" is not meant to be a derogatory title, but just an easier way to address substitutes as one may address "Mother" as "Mom."

If you are considering a career as a substitute (Doesn't just contemplating the possibility send a chill up your spine?), I strongly suggest you become known in one or two particular schools of your choice. If you work at any school that is assigned to you, then you expose yourself to the possibility of confronting anxiety attacks every time you go to a new school. This is because it entails dealing with a different secretary and principal each time, not to mention students who don't know you and who hope you are ripe for all their cute tricks.

Join me through the odyssey of a substitute teacher who could outsmart most any smart-ass student. In the ensuing chapters I will share with you some vignettes and antics which I have personally had the pleasure or displeasure of experiencing.

Seriously though, and I assure you at times I will be very serious, subbing does become easier when you are affiliated with only one or two schools because you might "almost," and I emphasize *almost*, be treated as a staff member.

This book is not intended to be an expose' on any particular school system, nor is it meant to denigrate any individual staff or student member of its system. It is simply meant to address a serious issue in a less serious fashion. Therefore, my purpose in writing this book is primarily to inform and entertain substitutes, new teachers and everyone else. I hope too that it will have universal appeal as we have all had experiences with substitute teachers. That should encompass almost everybody: parents, teachers and students of all ages. It seems to me that's nearly everyone in the world. I wish, I wish!

Chapter One

Reasons for Substituting

People become substitute teachers for numerous reasons. Some begin because they have not been able to find full-time employment as teachers and are hoping this will give them a foot in the door. Other people do so after they retire from teaching or other various careers and want a flexible job. Very often they are faced with a lot of free time, or they might want to escape their spouses who also have too much free time. Frankly, I find it a little strange, when, after teaching for twenty-five or thirty years, some people sign up to sub in the school from which they just retired.

For others, subbing is a way to enhance their income (not by much) and do something productive. But be assured that it certainly is not for the benefits it provides, because there usually aren't any. No sick days, no pension funds, and, if you happen to live in an area where there is a lot of snow, most systems will not pay you for the days you were booked in advance when school closes down for inclement weather. Have I discouraged you yet from becoming a substitute? If I haven't, then read on.

For me, it was a chance to earn extra income and to escape a very difficult time in my life. (Subbing certainly did distract me from my problems.) Although I had attempted other types of work, I always returned to some form of teaching. This is because I really do enjoy my association with children and because it keeps my spirit young and vibrant. Perhaps the reason for this is that most of my life I have felt like a big kid myself, and could relate so well to them.

Subbing is generally neither intellectually stimulating nor mentally challenging in the positive sense. You might be challenged, but that would probably be because you may have had a close encounter (of the unpleasant kind) with an aggressive student. Otherwise, to be quite candid, there are times when it can become utterly tedious. But, despite the negatives, there is often a certain amount of satisfaction derived at the end of the day. It's a great feeling knowing you have achieved law and order and the students have completed their assignments. Did you notice the above sequence of preferences for achievements? Discipline is a paramount issue.

Some school systems have tried using school administrators or other people who are not in the teaching field as subs. These experimental substitutes admitted it was one of the toughest jobs they have ever done and have come away with much more respect for subs.

On rare occasions when an emergency arises, coverage by staff members is a viable option. (Viable, but definitely not desirable.) However, there are some days when absenteeism is more rampant than others are, and coverage by teachers with free periods would never work. I have seen situations when a sub was called in at the last minute and a teacher had to cover the class. When the sub finally arrived one would have thought the teacher just discovered there was a Santa Claus.

The article in the Washington Post to which I previously referred suggested that the D.C. Schools, in order to comply with budget cuts, should eliminate substitute teachers except under certain circumstances when there was either a special emergency or when a long-term sub was required. The writer of the article obviously has wonderful insight and a working knowledge of a school system, because as the writer says, "While nobody pretends that a whole lot of mind expansion goes on when a substitute, with limited skills and near-zero notice, steps into a roomful of spontaneous predators," (Isn't that an interesting description?) "The response of a school system to absenteeism should not be to eliminate backups." Is the writer implying that subs are not too bright? I think not.

The D.C. school system, which is already in the midst of serious problems, wants to herd the students without their teacher, into the auditorium or foist them off on another teacher who teaches the same subject. Get real, people! As it is, classrooms are already overcrowded, which makes it almost impossible to be effective with such large groups and thus virtually eliminates any special attention a student might require. I know teachers will cringe at this possibility and I can already envision a chaotic situation with very resentful faculty members. Besides, it doesn't take much to aggravate teachers who have to deal with thirty-two or more students in each class. And in all honesty, who can blame them?

Speaking of coverage, an interesting situation arose when I was a full-time teacher in a small community in New Jersey where the principal of the high school was also the system's superintendent. Now that's a small system! As a music teacher in an elementary school, neither the art teacher nor I needed a substitute when we were absent. That school system, however, did not have an abundance of subs, so the art teacher and I were asked to substitute for the elementary school teachers. This happened at least two or three times. And if I recall correctly, (and I don't always), I believe the two of us complained bitterly about taking us away from our own work. First of all, we knew nothing about being elementary classroom teachers, and secondly, it diminished the importance of our own jobs.

That was my very first experience as a sub, which taught me back then to value their worth. However, my appreciation for subs was never as fervent as it is now, and as a result I am sitting down (it's hard to write standing up) and writing about my unforgettable experiences which I eagerly wish to share with you.

Some of them were positive and some were not. But my love for children overcame all the negatives associated with this job and helped me maintain a positive attitude. And if you too love children, your regard for them will provide you with a higher level of tolerance and a lower level of stress. I promise you it is essential to your well-being.

Chapter Two

Rules of Survival

In order to be effective as a substitute teacher, there are certain rules of survival of which you should be aware.

Rule number one: You must have a great sense of humor.

If you lack humor, you should at least have some masochistic tendencies. As a sub, you must understand you are not the "real" teacher. The "real" teacher lords the almighty grade over students. This statement comes directly from one of my private piano students who told me her class was mean to subs because "they can't do anything to us or give us a grade." Therefore, since you are not their "real" teacher, that makes you either a not-so-highly-paid baby-sitter or a lowly-paid police officer, detective, or prison warden. Once in a while, you might be an educated person who can answer the students' questions.

As a low-paid corrections officer, you are to maintain discipline by not allowing the students to kill each other even if at times it seems like a good idea; keep them from taking school property such as computers, books or erasers, etc.; watch out for cheaters, and dodge the flying missiles. Unfortunately, some of the schools to which you are assigned could have a few potentially dangerous students.

It is up to you to find out that information ahead of time and determine for yourself whether or not you want to deal with it. If you do, then it's probably because you are one of those people with the masochistic tendencies I was referring to earlier. If you decide you would like to be involved in this type of situation, imagine yourself going into battle, envisioning the school as a war zone. If the enemy happens to be friendly, then lucky you! I subbed in an excellent school and retired without any visible scars. Nevertheless, I did end my career with hypertension in lieu of a pension.

Yes, there will be times when you will feel like a highly-paid babysitter, but the truth is you are not, because sitters get at least five dollars an hour for watching one or two children. As a sub you might earn approximately twice that amount and be responsible for watching up to thirty-two or more children. By now, the sitter is probably earning ten dollars per hour while the sub is still waiting for a raise.

As a substitute, you must try to maintain order in a professional manner. Corporal punishment is a no-no. There is a law against that, as well as leaving a classroom unattended, so your presence is essential. There will, however, be days when you will feel like walking out on certain classes that are giving you a hard time. I strongly suggest that if you want to continue to be a sub, stay.

Understand that when students see a sub, they immediately speculate that the teacher left "busy work" and they don't have to do anything. They may also assume that if a test was scheduled, it was postponed. If it was not postponed then they will come up with, "Ms. Teech didn't want to be around to answer any of our questions about the test or listen to any of our complaints." Another common and inane remark I often heard was that their teacher either died or took a vacation. An evil look, or, "that's not funny" was generally my response. At any rate, they often make up bizarre stories as to why they believe their teacher is not in.

But no matter where their imagination leads them, some students are ready to greet you, the sub, with a few practical jokes. For instance, a student may walk into the class and unbeknownst to you, take the remote control for the video player. Suddenly, in the middle of taking attendance, you notice the video comes on without anyone being near it. At first you might think someone turned it on when the students came in, and so you nonchalantly turn it off. After a couple more times of this nonsense, you realize what's happened, especially when the giggling begins, and you start to look like a fool. This is where the sense of humor works.

Here you have three options. I've used all three. You can act perplexed and become flustered (those cute little sadists love that) or you can laugh with them and then warn them that if the remote is not returned, the whole class will have to pay for it. If you really want the students to enjoy your company, you will go totally ballistic by yelling and turning purple with anger, whereby everyone will get hysterical, and you at this point will fit those stereotyped concepts of "the sub," making you look like a real jerk. This manipulative ploy is used frequently in order to attempt to humiliate a sub. If you want to maintain your dignity, and I know you do, don't fall into that trap. Keep cool because once you've lost control they know they've got you, making it difficult for you to be taken seriously the rest of the time you're with them.

Incidentally, since that TV incident occurred, I have been informed by my teenage nephew that some students have a wrist watch with a remote control, universal to all TV sets. This answers the question as to why TVs keeps going on and off mysteriously. Isn't that cute? Now I'm thinking that before each class begins there should be a shake-down session, "OK guys, everyone hand over your watches!"

Rule number two: It's a good idea to be familiar with the subject for which you are subbing when you first start out. (I did.) This really throws the students off balance.

They would rather not have an instructional period when they are expecting to "party." However, in order to establish your credibility, a major challenge you must confront, I strongly advise that you sub primarily in your area of expertise and then slowly branch out into subjects you know nothing about! This is certainly a wiser strategy. Wow them with what you do know, so when the students ask you a question you can't answer you won't feel totally obtuse. You should also dispel any false illusions about entering a classroom, assuming you will get respect. (Rodney Dangerfield could relate to this job very well.) If you are an egomaniac and presume you are more intelligent than the students are, then stay away from a school environment. Low self-esteem works much better because children really believe subs are stupid. I remember being asked more than once if I had a degree in substitute teaching. The sad part is, the students weren't kidding, which made me wonder if they believe there is a college curriculum for dummies who can't be "real" teachers.

I realize that frequently throughout this treatise run strands of cynicism. But one must be realistic about the "plight of substitute teaching" because it is not recognized or assumed to be a "chosen" profession. One day I asked a class if I had inspired anyone enough to pursue a career as a substitute, and, as you probably can imagine, the class laughed, giving me the response I was expecting. Oh well, at least I have the satisfaction of knowing that when I was a full-time music teacher I was successful at instilling inspiration and enthusiasm to my students. (You'll have to take my word for it.)

In the meantime I am waiting for subs to hear the same accolades given to "Mr. Holland" and his Opus. Wouldn't that be a hoot, especially since I have done composing as well? DREAM ON, JUDY!!! (For those of you who are unfamiliar with "Mr. Holland's Opus", it's a movie about a composer who, in order to eat, takes a job as a High School band instructor. After successfully teaching and inspiring young people for over twenty-five years, he is forced to retire because the school budget has run out of money for the arts but not for the sports. All his students from the past show up at the school auditorium to honor him.) Of course, being a music teacher, this was a subject very close to my heart.

Now, my friends, if you're still hell-bent on becoming a substitute, please understand that the most important rule of all is rule number three. This rule stipulates that you must love children.

If you don't love children you should not be an educator, not even for a short term. It's not fair to you and it's definitely not fair to kids. Students cannot be fooled by an adult's sincerity or lack of it; they can always detect those who genuinely care about them. Since most children are spontaneous and honest they will quickly make a fair and usually accurate judgement as to the sincerity of a teacher.

A significant part of my life has been spent either interacting with children or educating them. I love being with them. I love talking to them. If you don't feel the same way, I urge you to do something else with your life.

Chapter Three

Your First Day at School

For those of you who have never been a substitute and are apprehensive about your first day on the job, set your fears aside while I share this unique and sometimes intimidating experience with you. I promise it will be a day you will never forget.

One morning, your phone rings and you are finally offered a substitute position that you eagerly accept. What I would like to prepare you for is an atmosphere that will probably be less than friendly. (I'm sure there are a few exceptions.) The aloofness you may encounter is due to the fact that the secretaries are dealing with attendance problems, phone calls, questions from students, questions from teachers, and edicts from the principal or assistant principal. In you walk, expecting them to be thrilled you're there. Although they might be happy to see you, don't expect applause when you arrive. Instead, you might be facing one of those busy secretaries who thinks *she* is the principal. She will probably be too stressed or too busy to explain the rudiments of taking attendance, showing you where your room is, or making sure you have a key to get into the room. (With no key, you might have to hold your classes in the hallway.) On my first day of subbing, I remember thinking that I wanted to go back home. Tough it out, dear hearts. You'll eventually get the hang of it. If I could do it, you can do it.

Being a new face in school can also be difficult when you come across a secretary who may appear to be intimidating, if she's not ignoring you. If you are not a teacher or a sub and are unclear about my description of the secretary/principal role, then perhaps you can equate it with the secretary/doctor role. The following story may clarify this description.

I called Dr. Wellthy one day to discuss a problem with him. His secretary informed me he was not in, and proceeded to ask me what my concern was. I, like a fool told her because I thought she would relay it to the doctor. Instead, she told me not to worry, and said if the problem still persisted after a couple of days, to call back. I asked her where she got her medical degree. The silence from her was deafening. I don't think she appreciated my sense of humor just as I did not appreciate her medical advice. However, I don't mean to pick on secretaries because most of them are valuable assets and quite competent. I just have a problem with those who think they are the bosses.

When the secretary finally gets around to giving you her divided attention, you better listen carefully to the instructions because she may not have either the time or the patience to repeat them. You may occasionally run into a friendly teacher, and if you're lucky, a friendly, seasoned sub who is familiar with the routine and will be able to give you a few helpful hints and unlock the classroom for you.

When you are unknown in a school, you should expect to be eyed as an extraterrestrial by the faculty. The reason for this is that very often some strange-looking subs come in posing as people. Without fail, when a teacher who has drawn one of these alien/subs, returns from his absence, he often discovers all hell broke loose while he was gone. I have a few ideas regarding the strange appearance of some of these subs, but first let me give you a quick pop quiz. Pick the answer you think fits best;

QUESTION—Do these people look weird because they
have been substitute teachers (a) too long, (b) not at

all (c) seldom (d) rarely (e) often, or (f) all of the above?

ANSWER—Any of these choices is correct. You may now proceed to the next section, to the topic of the main office and the aristocracy that reigns over it.

Principals fail to appreciate the presence of a substitute even more than their beloved secretaries do. Instead of greeting you with rose petals and throwing themselves at your feet for working in their school and doing a thankless job, they will more than likely ignore you. For whatever the reason, principals really seem to have no time for any formal niceties toward subs. There were few principals for whom I worked who knew me by name. Perhaps it's because I learned to maintain a low profile.

Instead of taking it as a personal affront, I came to realize that being ignored wasn't so bad. Keeping a low profile for a sub means staying away from the principal as much as possible. This warning stems back to my early days of subbing, when I encountered one of the nastiest principals I have ever had the displeasure of working for. I had a multi-day assignment at her school, and after the first day, I realized my classes did not begin until one hour after the bell rang. I was still a neophyte, and so I assumed I could come in a bit later. Wrong assumption! The Wicked Witch of the East found out my name and hunted me down for the kill. Principals can learn your name when they want to. Unfortunately it's not necessarily to compliment you for your good work. This woman laid me out unmercifully, implying that if I continued to come in late I would not be allowed to sub in the system again. Her meanness reminded me of an adage my father used: "You catch flies with honey, not with vinegar." I suppose this person never heard it. I chose never to go back to her school again, although later I learned she had moved on to a higher administrative position. Long live the witch! At least she can't harass children anymore, as mean witches usually do. I am also thankful that I was not a full time faculty member in her gingerbread house.

A word to the wise: Make sure you know ahead of time when you need to get to school and when you can leave. Since I had not had any kind of orientation or indoctrination, although that unkind principal did a pretty good job of it, I was not acquainted with arrival and departure times. (Not the ones at the airport, since going to a job like this is no vacation.) No one had told me we had to come to school a half an hour earlier than the students and hang around if we finished early making ourselves available for other tasks such as helping the secretary answer the phone or mopping floors (just kidding). Frankly, I can't see what that has to do with covering a teacher's duties, which is what most contracts stipulate. Remember, each principal is different, and although most of them require that you stay until the end of the day even when you finish early, there are some who don't care when you leave as long as you've successfully done your job. Of course, with the secretary/principal, it may be a different story. She might not like to see you leave early because she's probably jealous that she can't leave, even if she does make more money than you do.

Maintaining a low profile was also beneficial because there were, on various occasions, some ridiculous orders issued, concerning subs and passed along by "You Know Who." Yes, you are correct in assuming that You Know Who is the beloved, and sometimes not so beloved, secretary. These decrees were generally relayed to us like this; "Good morning, Judy." (Uh oh, what do they want? Good mornings are few and far between.) "Mr. Machismo wants you to know that all subs are to wear guest badges." Now really! I had been subbing almost every day for over eight years in the same school and I was there nearly as much, if not more than a lot of the faculty members. My question then was (1) Who is Mr. Machismo? (2) What does he look like? (3) Are those badges intended to make us look dorkier than the students already think we are? (4) Are we being discriminated against, and separated from the "real" teachers? (5) Are they

afraid we are potential killers? (Now there's a likely possibility!).
(6) Do they want us to be identified as guests, as opposed to
hosts in their school? What in the world is a host in school anyway?
(Certainly it is neither the secretaries nor the principal. They
had rarely been hospitable towards me. It's generally my nature
to be friendly, especially if someone seems to be bewildered and
in need of help, so I guess my mistake was in assuming I would
get the same treatment.)

The badge, which I refused to wear, might not have been
such a bad idea if it had our name and picture on it. But it merely
read "Guest." Now in all fairness to the school system, I must tell
you these badges were not meant to annoy subs like me, but
were used to protect the students from intruders who might pose
a potential danger. Everyone in school already knew me, which
was why I felt annoyed.

As a "regular" sub I was constantly asked by students and
teachers, "Who are you today?" For those of you who have never
been asked this asinine question a million times, it simply means
the person asking wants to know who you are subbing for that
day. I'm not sure why they cared, but I think they were just being
nosey because they never asked me how I was feeling. Even the
other subs got into the habit of asking each other that question.
It finally got to the point that I was asked, "Who are you today?"
so often, I began to lose my sense of identity and had to check
my driver's license to find out who I really was. That's where the
badge with a name and picture on it would have come in handy.
Can you imagine someone who is in the early stages of dementia,
being asked that question every day? Hey, now I know why some
of those alien-like subs looked so confused.

Another manifesto from the principal via the secretary was
that a sub be available to cover other classes during her free
period. We had not had a raise in several years, and people in
the cleaning service business were making more per hour than
we subs did. Now they expected us to be available to work on our
free periods! I repeat, keep that low profile, my friends.

I'm sure many of you subs have been issued some prize-winning edicts as well. The most ridiculous "orders from headquarters" I want to share with you was passed on to me by the secretary who was told by the principal that subs had to stay until two thirty, when in fact school ended at two o'clock. What were we supposed to do until then, hang around and pick our noses? Sorry, but I refused to do that too, especially since we were not getting paid for the additional half hour, and to my knowledge, no other principal had asked subs to stay. The school day had been extended an extra fifteen minutes, so according to my calculations, it added up to a cut in pay. And they expected me to stay longer? No way, Jose! Now I know what they mean when they say, life isn't fair. By the way, don't you find it amazing that the information was never given to us directly from the principal or written down as a memo? I certainly did.

There is no doubt in my mind that going to new schools can be awkward. I found that one of the most uncomfortable situations, (if you're shy you will relate to this) was being a new face in the teacher's lounge. Since I am on the reserved side with strangers, I felt ill at ease being there. I remember some of my first visits in the lounge when I did not know a soul. I would sit unspoken to, without anyone even nodding or smiling to acknowledge my presence in the "inner-sanctum." Someone suggested to me the reason teachers are so unfriendly to subs is because they are jealous of us and believe we don't need to work full-time. Well, I'm not sure about that. My theory is they presume they are on a higher level of professionalism than subs, or they are just too busy to be polite to strangers when they're grading papers or involved in their cliquey group. Not being pushy (to say the least), it took me two to three years to feel comfortable in faculty lounges.

Suggesting you keep a low profile conjures up an incident involving a principal and a substitute in an ugly situation. The story goes that a certain sub accepted a job only because the teacher had the last period off. The sub needed to leave early to get to a prearranged doctor's appointment. As providence would have it, another teacher also had to leave early and needed last-period coverage. Guess who was asked? If you answered, "the sub who had to leave early," you were right. Rumor has it there were heated words between the substitute and the principal when the sub refused to stay. The principal fired the sub (that's no rumor) and then sent a notice to the entire faculty instructing them not to call her again! The sub sued the school system, which in turn reprimanded the principal. She not only won her case, but also was reinstated and compensated for the days she did not work! Everyone at the school, except the principal and his secretary, approved of the outcome.

When you are "the new kid on the block," you might not feel comfortable asserting yourself, but as soon as you do get a foot in the door, try not to let yourself be taken advantage of. Those people who like to throw their weight around will do it when they think they can get away with it. New subs are an easy mark. Although it took me a long time to learn to say "no," when I finally did, I realized I was getting more respect. (Hey Rodney, there's the answer.)

Chapter Four

Lesson Plans

If you're reading this, I guess you weren't totally discouraged by Chapter 3 and you are still considering pursuing a career as a substitute. Frankly, the more I write, the more I feel ambivalent about encouraging any of you nice folks to go for it. I suppose it's because I don't want anyone putting a curse on me for recommending this profession. And if I seem to accentuate the negative and eliminate the positive, it's simply because I want to diminish the element of shock and surprise for you. After all, that is one of my objectives in writing this book.

So if you still decide you want to be a substitute, do so at your own risk. But be flexible, especially when you're dealing with lesson plans. Hopefully the regular teacher has left some plans and hopefully you are able to locate them, but there will be occasions when you literally have to hunt them down.

Sometimes when a teacher finds out he needs to be absent right before school starts, he may dictate the plans to the secretary over the phone. The secretary might inadvertently forget to give the plans to you after you've signed in, and still might not remember, until after you've torn the room upside-down looking for them. (Aren't secretaries supposed to be secretive?) If you've been resourceful enough to ask the secretary if she happens to know where the plans are hidden, she might say, "Oops, I forgot to give them to you," and go into her private drawer and come up with the lesson plans.

There are other good hiding places for lesson plans as well, such as the teacher's mailbox or with the department head. Occasionally the plans are never found. My guess is that when the plans are left on the teacher's desk, a student who wants to play a practical joke on a sub and watch him sweat, becomes a wanna-be magician, says "abracadabra" and makes them disappear.

Thus, to be a sharp sub you need good investigative skills. You might consider hiring Mike Hammer to train you, or I'll bet Mickey Spillane would appreciate your business. Anyway, when you locate the lesson plans, you may feel like you have won the lottery, particularly if the seating charts or attendance rosters are included. If they're both there, it's a double bonus.

Taking attendance is generally the first task of the day which is not as simple as you may think. "What's so hard about that?" you may ask. Well, since I'm sharing my secrets with you, I'll tell you.

Relying solely on seating charts for the attendance can be misleading. When students know a sub is coming, they often sit wherever they please in order to be near a friend with whom they can socialize. Even the most timid students become social butterflies when a sub is present. I wonder if it's because they imagine they see the word "stupid" written across our foreheads.

If you depend on seating charts and the students are not where they're supposed to be, you may mark the wrong people absent and call students by other students' names. They may giggle as they enjoy pretending to be the other student. Then when you think you're getting to know Debbie, someone will say "No, that's not Debbie, that's Lisa!" At that point, it's no use saying, "You should have told me." Another thing is when you call the roll, make sure there are as many names on the roster as there are students in the room. The students may answer for a friend who is not there. Now I'm not saying that children can't be trusted (yes, I am), it's just that they like to be cute and playful and they think cute and playful means making the substitute teacher look like a jerk.

When I did not receive class rosters or seating charts, I sent a blank sheet of paper around the room and had the students sign their names on it. I implore you to count heads, because some students may sign for an absent friend, making the number of names on the list different than the number of students in the room. That's because while you weren't looking, either someone sneaked out or Mickey Mouse or Elvis Presley surreptitiously sneaked in. Read the list and calmly remark that you don't see some of the famous people on the list, but if they were there, you certainly would be able to recognize Mickey and Elvis. Everyone can get a chuckle out of that and the kids will know you have not lost your sense of humor.

Don't fool yourself into thinking these shenanigans only take place in high school. There are some children in the elementary schools who also like to pull devilish pranks. I was told of a sub who came in to a fifth grade class on a long-term assignment for a teacher who was on maternity leave. The class did not know the sub was in for the rest of the year. When she took attendance, everyone switched names. This went on for several days until grades had to be entered in the grade book. At this point, the better-performing children, facing the prospect of getting someone else's bad grades, finally owned up to the class prank. Most of the poorer performing ones probably wanted it to continue.

What amazes me is how early in life children catch on to the phenomenon of causing trouble for subs. Could it be inherent? Perhaps it's in the DNA. Maybe scientists will do something about it after they're through cloning sheep and bringing back dinosaurs. Perhaps they'll start manufacturing sub-friendly children. Until then, I guess we'll just have to live with the species the way it is.

Getting back to the lesson plans: I want you all to know there is a world of difference between subbing for elementary school students and subbing for junior and senior high school students. Therefore, lesson plans are totally different for each level.

Today, "In This World of Ordinary People" and modern technology, many classrooms and homes are equipped with computers. Hopefully, the teacher will use the computer to type the lesson plans. Some of the handwritten ones may compel you to take a course in hieroglyphics to decipher them. I recall one teacher who printed the plans so small, I literally needed a magnifying glass to read them. When I finally did make them out, they were so useless that I realized why the teacher made them almost impossible to read. His department head, with whom I consulted, wasn't too thrilled with them either. I wasn't being a fink. I honestly couldn't understand what he wanted me to do.

Lesson plans can come in various shapes and forms, as do the teachers who prepare them. Some teachers give copious instructions, while others write merely a couple of concise lines. It gives you a clue about their personality. Although this does not usually reflect on their teaching ability, it can tell you if they are neatniks, disorganized slobs, or detail managers.

Although study periods in high school are common, study periods in elementary schools without structured activities are unmanageable. Can you imagine telling a group of six-or seven-year olds to find something to do or just study what their teacher had taught them the previous day? A seasoned sub (doesn't that sound like something you could sink your teeth into?) with elementary school experience, should know what to do if no plans are left or if the plans are not long enough to fill the day. You may be inclined to use the TV as a baby sitter, but that's a no-no. Sorry, you won't be able to let the kiddies watch your favorite soap operas. Come to think of it, you might both get something out of it if the networks would combine children's programming with your favorite soaps. Then you could all watch "Mr. Rogers' Dynasty" or "All My Barneys." It's just a thought. Anyway, you should probably bring an educational video or something you can show in a pinch.

Those of you who majored in elementary education probably picked up some helpful hints in those Methods classes. If you are not too old to remember them, you can use that background as a resource. Ingenuity on your part is essential. Use it before the children do, or else you will get a hard lesson on the real meaning of creativity.

At the high school level, teachers may ask you to show a video, give a test, or conduct a study period, or what the savvy students call "busy work." They use that term to make the work seem insignificant. Granted, at times it may be true, but often it is the same text book work the teacher gives for homework to reinforce what has already been taught. You know how much children "love" to do homework? Well, they love "busy work" even more. Students often resist doing it until you remind them they have to do it or else get a failing grade for the assignment. If that doesn't work, tell them that studies have shown that doing "busy work" enhances one's sex appeal. They probably won't believe you, but they'll at least appreciate your sense of humor.

When you're giving an assignment, you will probably hear, amid the moans and groans, the question "Can we work in groups?" This may mean they've arranged to have the class brainiac do all the work for everyone else to copy. It's a judgement call for you. It's O.K. for them to work in groups if you think it will be a genuine productive group effort. It's not O.K. if you believe a potential problem will arise. Again, it's a judgement call.

I was always delighted when the teacher wanted the class to turn in their assignment (It's the little things that make me happy.) because as I've mentioned, the responsible ones strived diligently to complete the work, while the not-so-ambitious ones slept or chatted.

One question you will definitely hear (you can bet your career on it) is, "What if we don't finish?" If I saw they had been working most of the period I would tell them they could take the work home and turn it in the next day. In such cases, the sub should leave a note for the teacher so the teacher won't think the students are lying when they said you told them they could take the work home. If the students did not even make an attempt to start the assignment, however, I would not permit them do it for homework either. Instead, I would insist they turn *something* in, even if it was a blank sheet of paper with their name on it. Students would often ask me why I cared if they did the work or not. I would reply that it was part of my job description, that I really cared about them, and that I was not there to make their life miserable unless they did it to me first.

Let me share two stories regarding lesson plans. The first incident happened to me personally, and the second to another sub.

My class was to take a practice test in preparation for an exam for the following day. (I had a three-day assignment.) The instructions stated that I was to give the students a practice test to work on individually. After twenty minutes they were to assemble in small groups and discuss their answers, and for the last five minutes, I was to read the answers from the answer sheet. Up to that point, the plans were great, and so was this class.

The teacher, however, neglected to leave a copy of the answers. The drama that followed resembled a Greek tragedy. The class carried on hysterically because, according to them, if they were unable to get the answers to the practice test, how could they possibly take the real test? Some students could have been nominated for an Academy Award for their superb acting. I reminded them this was only a review of material which had already been taught. I could see this was a popular ploy used to postpone a test. Being a musician, I know how to improvise, so I let them read their answers aloud and told them to assume the answer most often given would hopefully be the correct one. It worked!

The second incident involved another "regular" sub who was asked, before she left the building, to cover for a teacher who had to be taken to the hospital for an unspecified amount of time. The hospitalized teacher contacted her on the phone while she was still in school and requested that she come to the hospital to pick up the plans so he could go over them in detail with her. When she declined, he slammed the phone down in her ear. She happens to be a little deaf, but that she heard. I often wondered how this lady kept so calm under the most adverse conditions until I learned about her hearing problem. Boy, that's got to be advantageous for subs. Mind you I'm not recommending making yourself deaf, but let's face it, you can't get upset with crackling kiddies or temperamental teachers if you can't hear them.

Even if you sincerely intend to adhere to the plans, extenuating circumstances might prevent you from doing so. You see, both these incidents occurred on the same day as a bomb scare. This sick prank kept everyone waiting outside in the cold for an hour and a half while the K-9 crews went in. No bomb was found. There were rumors about who pulled the prank, but to my knowledge the culprit was not caught. I thought it was probably a student who wanted more time to study for a test. Or, I thought perhaps the secretary who answered the phone didn't hear the message correctly. The caller might have said there was a "bum" in the building. When everyone finally returned to the classrooms, someone started a small fire in one of the girls' bathrooms, which in turn made the natives even more restless for the remainder of the day.

With so many major disruptions, the trick is for a sub to carry out lesson plans with aplomb, which by no means is an easy task, even for regular teachers. Flexibility is the key, requiring you to make adjustments accordingly. How?

One of the easiest methods for a change of plans in the upper grades is to let the students use the time as a study period. Now, when you tell them "study period," somehow they hear "time to socialize." Conscientious students might actually study, but the rest will goof-off. If they get too rambunctious, you may have to sit on them. Like a baby sitter, I mean. In any case, don't take the goof offs' behavior personally because they behave the same way for everyone.

There is another common lesson plan besides the "busy work" one which I would like to prepare you for. It is the film or video time-killer. Teachers leave that when they cannot think of anything more constructive or creative. Occasionally the video is used as a teaching tool, either to enhance a previously taught lesson, or to present new material. That's good, because the class might have a work sheet to complete after watching the film, which means they have to pay close attention and perhaps take notes. At least that's productive. But often a teacher will leave a film that is totally unrelated to the current course work and the students, between napping, will swear they've seen it five times. Well, you may have to watch it five times in one day, which is why I have to warn you about it.

Many students use video time as an excuse to party. You will become aware of this when they may request and even insist you turn off all the lights, saying there is a glare or they can see better with the lights out and the blinds closed. Beware! Experience has taught me not to be too trusting, especially if I didn't know the class with whom I was dealing. Lights out is often taken as a signal for the launching of pencils, candy, or missiles across the room. Despite the darkness, they'll always manage to hit you, like they've got radar or something. And then they'll say it was an accident!

During one of those famous video periods, a noteworthy incident arose involving another sub, who was going to show a video. He left the VCR unattended while he was taking roll. Nothing wrong with that, right? Wrong! Someone switched the video when he wasn't looking and when he turned it on, a porno film came on. (No, it was not a sex education class.) How's that for a practical joke?

First of all, why would a student bring a porno film to school? Maybe I'm a little paranoid, but I think perhaps the student was waiting for a sub to be in one of his classes when a video was on the agenda. That indicates how often students expect to watch films when their teachers are absent. Somehow, they always seem to find out during the course of the day, via the grapevine, when they will be having a sub, who the sub will be, and what they will be doing.

Thank God I was not their sub that day. I've had more than my share of practical jokes pulled on me, but none quite that bad.

One day I was subbing in the Physical Education Department. The teacher left a film for an aerobics class. The machine needed to be rolled from the office to the auxiliary gym, so I did that prior to the start of the class in order to begin promptly after taking roll. Since I'm no Jane Fonda, just pushing the machine was strenuous enough for me! It was also a good excuse for not participating in any of the aerobic exercises, especially since I hate that stuff.

When it came time for me to run the tape, I discovered the VCR was not working. Three girls approached me, eager to help me find the problem. Little did I know they had caused the problem in the first place. (Another student squealed on them.) They soon pointed out a broken connection. (How astute of them!) I had checked the VCR earlier and it was working perfectly fine. By the time I got someone to fix it, the class was just about over—PARTY TIME!!!

Believe it or not, similar incidents happened to me two more times. I'm not sure if it's because I was too trusting or I have a short memory or that I am a slow learner. (Then again, what can you expect from a person who gets poison ivy every year because she forgets to wear long sleeves when picking weeds, or who sprays bleach while wearing dark clothes? I tell everybody those pretty pink spots are to decorate a drab navy blue or black outfit.)

I never let the VCR out of my sight again. It became attached to me like Velcro. There went my trusting nature, and my reputation as Mrs. Nice Guy!

One of the most annoying video lesson plans I've ever dealt with was The "Star Wars" trilogy left by an instrumental music teacher. Mind you, each class is forty-five minutes long, so even though I was there for three days, I was still unable to get through all three films, which take over six hours to watch. I guess he wanted me to be prepared in case we were snowed in for a week (in May). Popcorn and sodas were the only things missing.

I don't know what this teacher was thinking or if he was just plain lazy, but if he had given the plans some thought, I'm sure he could have come up with something more interesting and more musically oriented. Sometimes I'm not sure who he was irritating more, the students or the sub. Just being in that room with no windows and poor ventilation was difficult enough. Did he have to punish everyone for his absence? Each time a class came in, they would moan and cry, "May the force be with you" when they caught a glimpse of the "Trilogy."

This teacher left the "Star Wars" trilogy for all subs every time he was out, not just me—and the class got real tired of it. One day the tapes mysteriously disappeared. It was my belief that a student probably hid them so the classes wouldn't have to watch them again. Actually, I even entertained the idea myself. The day the teacher returned to school he was unable to locate the tapes. I immediately got a call from him asking if I knew what had happened to them. I was concerned as to their whereabouts, but I must admit, I was also half-relieved. NO MORE TRILOGY! Maybe now the class can watch "Mr. Holland's Opus" a few dozen times. At least that's about a music teacher.

If by chance you are wondering why as a music teacher I did not rehearse either the choral or instrumental groups in all the times I was requested to sub for those classes, I have a good explanation.

Unless you are a great sight-reader or your name is Leonard Bernstein, it is too risky for a sub to try to be the conductor when you are totally unfamiliar with the music or the students. Quite often, a competent music student can suffice because he or she will likely gain the cooperation of the class sooner than would a sub. If that proves not to be the case, then step in. I remember one girl who yelled at the class so loudly that she became hoarse.

"I know how you feel," I whispered to her, as I gave the class one of my evil stares.

Once, early in my subbing career, I tried to conduct a band— and the students all switched instruments on me. Not only was that humiliating, but it sounded, like a bunch of dying animals. I was almost ready to give up my title of "music teacher."

I want to end this chapter on an upbeat note and tell you about the nicest lesson plans I had ever received. Oh, I forgot what the plans were about, but on top of them were a thank you note and a bar of candy. Sweets for the sweet! I remember all the nice stuff too.

Chapter Five

Student Preferences for Subs

Most students have their favorite subs, and quite often the title of "Favorite Sub" was bestowed upon me. (Mrs. Mehr, Queen of the Subs. An honor I dreamed about all of my life.) Though I sound sarcastic, those kudos made my job gratifying and made me feel loved. Actually, there were kids who used to tell me they loved me, and I know they weren't trying to butter me up either. One year, two senior boys asked me to go to their prom. I was very flattered, but luckily, I had to be out of town. Honest! Then there was the boy who would sing, "Did I ever tell you you're my hero?" every time he saw me. These were the types of things that reinforced my positive association with young people. (They know quality when they see it.)

When and if the children like you, the job can be rewarding (perhaps that's a slight exaggeration) or at the very least, enlightening. First of all, they will feel free to gossip to you about their teachers. They'll tell you who they like or dislike or which of them are good instructors or not so good instructors. I often heard kids say, "Mr. Smarty really knows the subject matter, but he can't teach it to us." You also get to hear some juicy stories about some of the staff members, which you might not otherwise hear. This is the "enlightening" part. It always amazes me how some teachers share some private and personal aspects of their lives with students. Personally I don't think it's a good idea to reveal anything to kids because they are born gossips and stories get circulated quickly.

One such story was told to me by one of the school's leading gossip, who enjoyed chatting with teachers and asking them personal questions. By his indiscretions of divulging other people's business, I knew he was not to be trusted with the time of day. Anyway, the story goes, that a divorced teacher, who often spoke unkindly of kids, imparted to the school yenta that he liked his dog more than he liked the women he dated because women took advantage of him and his generosity. He would buy them expensive presents such as diamond rings and they in turn would dump him. You must be wondering how this man could afford such extravagant gifts on a teacher's salary. I was told he had an outside business in addition to his teaching and earned over $100,000 a year. Perhaps if he had spoken a little nicer about kids and women, I might have been interested in him, but I believe he should confine his relationships exclusively to dogs.

Of course, what the students convey is only hearsay and their opinion. Although they seem to have a sixth sense about their teachers, it tends to be biased. However, I know that when a malicious rumor concerning a teacher gets started, it perpetuates itself year after year. I remember they used to accuse one particular teacher of being an alcoholic because she had rosacea, a blood vessel problem on her nose. They assumed she was always intoxicated, when I know in fact she was not. She finally retired (soberly), and I firmly believe it was because she got tired of hearing the rumor. Anyway, I have since seen her teetering around the mall, happy as a lark singing, "No more pencils, no more books, no more students, dirty looks."

On a positive note, I have had students confide in me concerning their family life or their future college plans. After hearing so many family problems, I am now convinced that almost every teenager could use some psychotherapy. You'd be amazed how many kids claim they hate their parents. But I know most kids don't; they just say it to relieve their frustrations.

When they were indecisive about their college plans, they actually asked me to help them make up their minds as to which college they should attend. Usually it was because they wanted to go to one school and their parents wanted them to go to another. Naturally I was flattered, but I didn't have to pay their tuition, thank God, and I am not really a mavin in college counseling. (OK! I admit I don't know everything.) Occasionally, I would give them some input, but how much could I know about their personal needs when I had spent only a few hours a year with them?

Many times students are happy to see almost any sub simply because it's a break in the routine. If it's a sub they like, it is probably because they think that person is "cool." That of course does not translate into letting them get away with anything, although I know of one particular sub who would give the students some of the answers to a test, or completely ignore the lesson plans and talk about her life growing up in The Big Apple. The students thought she was the "coolest," and since they also tend to blab a lot about what goes on, the teachers found out about her subbing techniques and consequently she was rarely asked to sub again, except out of desperation.

If you are subbing for the first time and this is your initiation in a classroom without supervision, e.g. as a student teacher, keep in mind that you must maintain an aura of authority. If you appear to be intimidated by an unruly class, you will surely become a target for their cute pranks. Don't be afraid of being disliked. You may not even want them to like you, and so I suggest that in the beginning of a school year you do not smile a lot, and try to appear stern and strict. You can always lighten up later. Don't worry, because eventually your true nature, good or bad, will manifest itself.

Those students who give the sub a hard time are invariably the same ones who are difficult with their own teacher. That being the case, you should exert a certain amount of authority without being overly rigid. The natives could become rebellious and then you won't be having any fun. Learn to maintain a balance. I used the tactic of not smiling when the students didn't know me. I realized that at times I appeared to be a grouch, but looks are often deceiving and those students for whom I had subbed on previous occasions, knew what a pussycat I was, with an acerbic tongue. I only feigned this seriousness for those who tried to see how much they could get away with. And, kids will constantly test you. The truth is that I was hardly ever grouchy; although there were times I had to bite my tongue in order not to laugh at some of their silly antics. I used the sober-faced tactic as a defense mechanism. It gave me a sense of having the edge over any of the pranksters. And believe me when I assure you there are plenty of smart alecks around. Once they recognized I was shrewder than they were, I eased up on my serious demeanor and became a friendlier person, sarcasm and all. It did work for me! I urge you to develop a strategy with which you are comfortable and go with what works for you. You too can become someone's favorite sub.

Chapter Six

Teacher Preferences for Subs

I presume that every school system has its own way of contacting substitutes. Some schools have their beloved secretaries call the subs. Some schools require that the teachers themselves find a sub and of course, now we have the most modern method—computer calls (at 5:30 A.M).

Aren't you already annoyed, knowing what it's like to deal with automated computer calls? They are so impersonal and frustrating, you can grow old waiting to talk to a real person! But many people look at me as if I'm crazy when I dare to suggest doing away with computers (except for word processing) and going back to using our brains. When computer systems go down, the world appears to become immobilized and workers are clueless about their jobs. Our society has become so dependent on computers that eventually people will become inconsequential. Before you know it, when you need to talk to your psychotherapist, you will make a call to her office and you might just hear this, "If you are a schizophrenic, press 1, If you are a manic-depressive, press 2, neurotic, 3", etc., etc. Every once in a while, the recorded therapist can throw in a "how does that make you feel?" or "tough it out." Hey, maybe I'll start a 900 dial-a-therapist phone number. It could be more lucrative than being a sub.

Before I begin to discuss teachers' preferences for subs, let me explain to you how this computer system operates. The telephone rings, you say "hello" and what you hear might remind you of a "Mission Impossible" directive. "This is the Hollywood County School System calling for (my voice) "Judy Mehr." We have a position available for you. If you want to hear it, press 1." (Of course I want to hear it, dummy.) "If you decline this position, press 9." Even if I had a job for that day, I was dying to know who was going to be absent and didn't call me personally. The computer also informs you when you have been requested, which is always a nice thing to hear. There are other options as well, but I'm sure you've got the idea. So let's get back to the business of discovering why some teachers have their preferences, and how you can become a "regular" sub.

If you like a certain school, and it likes you, try to get on the preferred list. (A sub can be an elitist too.) A little schmoozing never hurts. Take advantage of opportunities to suck up to the secretary, when she can spare the time to talk to you. Inform her of your availability and tell her how much you like working in "her" school. When the secretary is in charge of locating subs, teacher preference does not make much of a difference. At times though, the teacher might request that the secretary call the teacher's preferred sub.

You may wonder why a teacher may have a preference for a certain sub. God only knows. Although I will try to answer the question, I promise you, I don't profess to be "God."

There are a few teachers who don't care who comes in for them as long as they have coverage. Then there are those teachers who use only one person despite the fact the sub may not know a blessed thing about the subject matter. I believe this is where chemistry between two people becomes a factor. In such cases, the teacher will rearrange his or her schedule in order to use the preferred sub. Teachers often arrange a day which he terms "a mental health day," to avoid having a nervous disorder. Another reason a teacher prefers a certain sub is because he knows the sub is familiar with his own routine, knows he can depend on that person to carry out his plans, and can take attendance accurately.

(Each school has its own attendance system, and unless it is done properly, the attendance secretary will have a conniption! So will the student if he was marked absent when he was really in class. It is therefore a good policy to follow up on a student who may have cut a class. The teacher appreciates it, and the student will learn that he will not be able to cut the next time you are his sub.)

I know that in all the years I was in one school, there were a few teachers who rarely asked me to sub for them. If and when they ever did, the conversation went something like this,

"Hi Judy, this is Joe Doe. I was looking for a sub for next Friday. Can you come in for me?"

Me—"Sorry but I'm booked for that day."

Joe Doe, "Gee, I've already called everybody else and they're booked too. What's going on?"

(As you can see, tact is not always a teacher's forte.) Being informed that I was his last choice did not make me feel loved. In fact, *chicken liver* might be descriptive of my feelings. If I got the impression I was called out of desperation and I didn't already have a job, I would decline the position. I do have some pride and dignity.

I once received a call from the computer to sub for one of those teachers who never before called me. (You can assume she has poor taste.) On the day I was requested, several teachers were scheduled to attend a seminar. (Seminars are times when some very strange subs creep into the system.) I was taken by surprise that she had not requested someone else, but I accepted the assignment. Later, I found out my initial instinct was correct.

The day after I accepted the job, another teacher asked me to sub for her for that same day. When I told her I was subbing for Plain Jane, she informed me it wasn't possible because Barbara was coming in for Jane. She knew that because she had asked Barbara herself. That evening, Jane called to inform me she was not certain she would be attending the seminar since the administration had not yet approved her leave. I knew that wasn't true because assignments for each faculty member had been designated two months earlier, and each teacher was required to attend. I ended up switching to the other person who asked me, because she at least was honest enough to admit she had asked another sub first and me second.

To add insult to injury, the teacher who lied to me stopped me in the hall at school the day before her absence to let me know she had just gotten administrative approval to attend the seminar. I was faced with the fact that not only did some students lie to me and think they could get away with it, but a few teachers did as well. Give me a break, guys. I'm not as stupid as I may look! Although I was tempted to embarrass her with the truth, I kept my mouth shut, not an easy task. So, whenever I ran into Jane, I was tempted to shout, "Liar, liar, pants on fire." (You pick up stuff like that being around kids all day.) The only thing that stopped me was a little voice in my head reminding me that I am a mature (?), middle-aged woman who needs to act with decorum.

Another common snafu in the computer system was one in which two subs came in for the same position. If you want to see annoyed people, boy, those subs were really ticked. Especially the one who didn't get the job. (How would you like to be awakened at five-thirty in the morning, show up at school only to find out you didn't have the job you expected?) At times like that, the teacher with the job number got to work. Sometimes the school would offer to pay the extra sub to stay and do clerical work. Oh, the joys of those computer errors!!!

Here's another one of my memorable gems. I had accepted a job from a department head who had planned to take a day off one week in advance. As it happened, I had to cancel the assignment because I needed to go out of town in order to take care of an emergency. (Emergencies do arise, even for subs.) I explained my situation to her, giving her three days notice so she would be able to find another sub. I remember she sounded annoyed, but I thought she understood. Wow, was I wrong! I found out later that she ordered everyone in her department never to call me again because I "wasn't reliable." Not reliable! In eleven years, I canceled a job less than three times.

I believe four years went by before she asked me to sub again, although a couple of times the computer requested the honor of my presence to fill in for her. Just for spite I took the job! (I can be vindictive too.) She even feigned relief when she found out I was her sub. I learned not to take this person seriously when I knew she would talk to her students about her boyfriends and her dates, and who once bared her breasts wearing a bunny outfit in a faculty lounge for a colleague's birthday. Nevertheless, I always found it amusing when she announced in my presence that she needed a sub and proceeded not to ask me. Sensitivity was not one of her strong points. Isn't human nature fascinating?

There is one more reason why some teachers pick one sub over another. After several years, word got out to me that a form of payola was going on in the school by certain subs. A teacher confided in me one day that she rarely took off from school, but when she did she used Ms. Crafty because of guilt feelings. It turned out Ms. Crafty was in the habit of giving certain teachers Christmas presents, which made them feel obliged to use her when they were absent. I must confess I was somewhat shocked because this woman appeared to be a Miss Goody-Two-Shoes, but I guess when it comes to money, some people can justify anything. The irony of all this is that I'd heard her use the word "greedy" in reference to people who subbed a lot. Wasn't she the one who was being greedy, giving the teachers gifts?

I can honestly admit I got jobs strictly on my merit and my fabulous personality. (Who said I had to be humble?) I never gave anyone the impression they were obliged to ask me to sub and I think giving presents was a little tacky and not playing the game fairly. Even some teachers thought it was a strange gesture. *C'est la vie.* I shouldn't be surprised by what people do anymore, but can you believe it could be a dog-eat-dog world in the subbing field? As strange as it may sound, there are actually some people dying to have our jobs.

Besides greed, childishness also factors in. I remember when another sub remarked about a job I took. He informed me he was unable to accept it, because his datebook had been filled for the entire next week. I suppose it was his way of showing superiority by announcing he was asked first. Children aren't the only ones who feel they have to be the most popular kid in school.

I recommend that if possible you sub regularly at only one school. It worked for me, and most of the faculty treated me with consideration, appreciation and respect after years of working with them. If they had not, you can be sure I wouldn't have lasted there as long as I did.

Chapter Seven

Chemistry in the Classroom

We have often heard that children from other countries are so much more polite and respectful than American children. I have seen children in classrooms from almost every part of the world, and the fact of the matter is they are virtually all the same because human nature is universal. The renowned psychologist, Carl Jung, termed it the "collective unconscious," potential ways of behavior common to all human beings. In the framework of this chapter, Mehr calls this "collective unconscious," the "rotten kid syndrome." In some way, almost every child possesses it, and when you get two or more children together, some weird chemical reaction happens.

I mean it when I say "chemical" reaction. In science, a chemical reaction is a change in the composition of matter into something quite different from the original ingredients. Through my own observations, I have posited that when certain children interact, something happens chemically in their brains resulting in the "rotten kid syndrome".

This chemical reaction takes place in every classroom and can be quite difficult to appreciate when the chemistry does not emit favorable results. (Ergo, "the rotten kid syndrome.") Since I profess to be an aficionado of the science of psychology and I may even consider myself a pseudo-psychologist, I will attempt an explanation of this phenomenon from my own point of view. In order to explain it properly, I need to acquaint you with the fundamentals of how classes are frequently constructed.

A class is generally formed by using a random combination of students. At a Junior or Senior High School, this randomness is affected by the needs of course scheduling.

At elementary schools, it is likely that a random number of students are brought together either homogeneously or heterogeneously. (Aren't you impressed by the fact that subs know these big words too?) I will take an educated guess that when a class is formed homogeneously, the randomness is narrowed down.

In either case, there is always a chemical factor to be scrutinized. Whoever coined the adage "One bad apple can spoil the basket," must have been a teacher. Picture this scene: A class of third-grade students is having an art lesson in fingerpainting. Everyone is doing what he or she is supposed to except the proverbial "Little Johnny." "Johnny" decides that he doesn't want to use the paper he was given, but now he is ready to extend his creativity to painting his face or the back of one of his classmate's shirt as well. Up to this point, the lesson is going smoothly until another child spots "Johnny." "Rotten kid syndrome" kicks in and now every child is giggling hysterically and imitating "Johnny." What seemed like a fun learning experience has turned into a hellish session. I am certainly an advocate of creativity and fun, but trust me when I tell you that those kinds of experiences are not very humorous.

I have subbed in a few art classes, and I want you to know if you are not an art teacher, it is probably the hardest class to sub for. (Sorry about that, Art Teachers of America!) This is because there is so much cleaning up to do! Unless you don't mind acting as a custodian, I suggest you either do not take the assignment or just use it as a study period. Students seem to trash the room more than usual in the name of art. In which case, most of them will not do anything productive, so why bother with a big mess?

I don't mean to sound negative but I want you to know what one may be facing when taking on an art assignment.

I had a cute experience in my early days of substituting when I only substituted in my subject matter. Remember I was a music teacher and remember also, that I strongly recommended that you stick with your area of expertise in the beginning of your subbing days? It's a good way to get your feet wet.

I arrived at an elementary school one cold day in January with a child's biography of early Mozart. I remember it was in January because it was Mozart's birthday. I also brought some records with me. (Do you remember what records are? They were those old black round things that spun around a turntable and played music.) In any case, I was totally confident that the children would love the lesson. This biography began with Mozart when he started composing music at age three. (I wouldn't be surprised if he was one of those little precocious brats, who suffered from the "rotten kid syndrome" himself.) I was totally under the impression that the children could relate to this composer since he was close to their age.

At that point, I was unaware of the vast differences between "teacher" and "sub" until my first class of the day. They were an adorable group of second grade munchkins. As soon as they stepped into the music room, whispers of "sub, sub" permeated throughout. I thought to myself, "Isn't that cute?" Being an old pro, I was not worried about handling the situation. Besides, I was a lot bigger than they were, and I wasn't about to let a bunch of seven-year-olds intimidate me. When they were seated, I taught them a little song by which they could introduce themselves. I would sing "What's your name?" and they in turn would sing their names back to me. (By this means, I would immediately remember everyone's name; and if you believe that, then I've got some other good stories for you.) Very often, children were too shy to respond, in which case I did not embarrass them by insisting they sing.

After the introduction, I told the children that it was Wolfgang's birthday. (The name Wolfgang always brought a few chuckles), and that he was actually younger than they were when he began to play the clavier (piano) and compose music. While I was giving the class some background information, one little girl who was as cute as a button kept upstaging me by talking and acting silly. In such situations, I usually stopped what I was saying and waited for the talking to cease.

(Some high school students termed this annoyed stare as "THE LOOK," an annoyed stare that was better than Lauren Bacall's. Silence is a very good attention-getter, and children instinctively know how irritated you are. Sometimes they stop and listen and sometimes they don't.)

In this case, the chatter finally subsided, and I completed the background information and asked them if they wanted me to read the story of Mozart to them. Big mistake! Never give a class the option of a refusal when you have a lesson prepared. By the way, the teacher had left me no plans that day, and luckily I came prepared.

Almost everyone in the class shook their heads to the affirmative except the cute "little button." In a loud clear voice she shouted, "No." The children went into hysterics, and I got my first real taste of what being a sub was all about. I was truly flabbergasted to think this child had the audacity to say "no" and the rest of the class thought she was funny. Didn't they realize I was supposed to be the only one who could make jokes? I guessed not. I was convinced this type of behavior occurred because I was not their regular music teacher. That must have been the beginning of my paranoia as a sub. The cute little second grader threw me completely off balance, (Rotten Kid!) but I survived, and the rest of the day went pretty much without incident. Anyway, the point I am trying to make is how easily one small little tot can disrupt an entire classroom. All twenty-five children reacted to her instead of paying attention to me. Maybe I was just jealous, but I wouldn't be surprised if one day she becomes a stand-up comedian.

It's funny how early in life children learn not to take subs seriously. A colleague of mine told me that when she told her family she was going to be a substitute teacher, her eight-year-old son began to whine and told her not to be one because he didn't want them doing "that" to her. I believe "that" was synonymous with substitute abuse. Isn't that a charming story? No, it's not, but it is a fact of sub life.

Now, let us examine a situation in which there is more than one disruptive troublemaker in a class. Two friends, Carrie and Kelly have a notoriously bad reputation individually because they are both loud and obnoxious. (I really hate to use the word obnoxious so freely and so frequently, because somewhere out there, there are parents who supposedly adore them. At least, I hope they do.) These two are the same students who walk in the halls speaking at deafening levels. Their voices literally can be heard down the hall and in the next room. They truly think this behavior is acceptable and cannot believe that anyone dares to insinuate they are speaking too loudly or has the temerity to ask them to lower their voices by three decibels. After all, they may ask, what are they doing that is so terrible? Once again, my paranoia leads me to believe this poor conduct is in honor of the substitute, and is meant to prime the class for "party time." This is not a difficult task. These two young ladies (and I use the term loosely) would make great social directors on a cruise ship since they are so good at inspiring others to have fun, fun, fun.

Somehow, these not-so-cute loudmouths always manage to find each other, and end up sitting on the same side of the room. I have seen it happen so often, I must postulate that it is more than a coincidence. Fate has forced them together, on their teacher, and on the sub. (The Gods must be playing folly with student placements!) The room almost seems to be magically divided into two sections, with the workers and quieter students on one side, and the drones and queen bees on the other side. I have often wished I could record all of this on a hidden camera. Allen

Funt's "Candid Camera" show would have had a ball airing some of those precious moments.

This is the exact kind of chemistry I am referring to. It begins in the kindergarten, (possibly even in nursery school) and invariably continues through to High School graduation. Not having taught at the college level, I can only assume this sort of behavior is not tolerated there. However it probably does go on in college dorms or frat houses, where one hears about beer guzzling and outlandish behavior taking place. I will not attempt to give you a scientific explanation as to the chemistry taking place. But I assure you that whatever chemistry exists, it is amplified and exaggerated to the max in the presence of a sub.

I could also discuss how "good" chemistry transpires as well, but what could I say sarcastically about positive chemistry or good behavior? Probably not very much except that it does exist, in which case this book might end up being only ten pages long. However, there are a lot of good students out there, and they are the ones who make the teaching profession gratifying. Nevertheless, I really believe we learn the best lessons from negative situations.

Now, in all fairness to the students, understand that at times, obnoxious subs creep into the system. They are the subs who instill animosity in students because they don't know the first thing about handling children in a classroom situation. These subs are the ones who will undoubtedly get pencils and/or spitballs thrown at them. When the whole class is unhappy with one of these kinds of subs, even the well-behaved kids might join in on inappropriate behavior and laugh at the pranks being played on the sub. This is known as "comic relief" at the expense of the sub. Generally there is a lot of histrionics taking place, making the students even happier. As you can imagine, not everyone is cut out for teaching.

But in spite of the fact I keep saying you should NEVER lose your sense of humor, I have occasionally lost mine. After all, we subs are human, and if you've ever seen us at the end of a school day, you would swear the system had employed a bunch of zombies. Frankly, there are occasions when you've had such a rotten day that it is virtually impossible to maintain that sense of humor. And, for some strange reason, human nature allows us to remember more negative situations than positive ones, which as I've commented before, makes for far more interesting reading matter and storytelling.

(Have you ever read through an entire newspaper or listened to a newscast where ALL the news is good? People do not seem to listen as attentively to the good stuff as much as they do to bad news or sensationalism. Actually, I've thought of printing a newspaper or having a TV show reporting only good news. It has got to bring positive results to our society and to children who are so impressionable. Children learn by imitation, and if they were exposed to more constructive situations, there's the possibility of less crime in this world!!)

Nonetheless, it's still the negative incidents I reflect on with both humor and frustration which reinforces the fact that I don't miss subbing, although I do miss my interactions with children.

I know at times I tend to be redundant (that's a nice word for a NAG), but I want to be sure that you do not go into substituting for frivolous reasons such as, "this job is a cinch," or "it will tide me over until I find something better." That just won't do, because going into subbing unprepared can bring only misery into your life, and who in his right mind wants to go to a job to be miserable? Masochists, of course. Now that I think back, I too must have fit into that masochistic category to a certain degree because I kept going back for more and more abuse!

One of the most negative recollections of undesirable chemistry involved practically an entire grade of teenagers. It was the first year the high schools in my district brought in ninth graders. Up until then, high schools included only grades ten through twelve, and in those days we all thought how immature the tenth graders were. I had forgotten how young middle-school students acted since I had not been involved with that age level for many years.

If you are either a parent or a teacher and have dealt with children in the twelve to fourteen-year-old age group, then you are probably familiar with Haywire Hormones, which I am sure is one cause of "rotten kid syndrome." Trust me, my friends, when I tell you how the adolescent hormonal changes that take place are absolutely amazing! Symptoms include silliness, giggling, zits, an attraction to the opposite sex, and the belief that at their age, they have really become adults. They believe they are ready to branch out on their own and declare their independence. That is, until they need spending money, then see how quickly they revert back to childhood. Far be it from me to lop off any of those branches, unless of course they become too overgrown, because teenagers certainly do need to evolve and assert their individuality. My only desire was for them to lose the attitude of, "I know all the ways to annoy a teacher, and especially the substitute."

Because I'm a cockeyed optimist, I never would have believed that practically an entire ninth grade class could give me such a pain in the butt. Because of them, I entertained the idea of giving up the teaching profession to write about my experiences in order to warn others before it was too late.

I began to believe I had actually been abducted by aliens from another planet and forced to work for them. Granted, there were some exceptions, but they were few and far between. I knew in my heart that I would have felt guilty if I were the only teacher with such negative opinions. But the truth is, it was the general consensus of not only the substitutes, but of the entire faculty. This intolerable behavior continued throughout their four years in high school.

I remember being constantly on the verge of not subbing anymore. But extenuating circumstances prevailed and so I stuck it out like the trooper that I am. (Actually, I needed the money because my family has the bad habit of liking food.) But without a doubt, it was by far, the worst year I had ever spent dealing with teenagers who were both spoiled and ornery. That was the time when I had ALMOST lost my sense of humor!!! Just to give you an example of one of those horrendous experiences, I'll tell you about an incident, which stands out, so vividly in my mind.

It was the last period of the day, (Last periods seem to be more memorable than others.) and I was subbing in a ninth grade Spanish I class, a language in which I am fluent. The teacher had left some good lesson plans, which entailed completing a few pages in their workbook for the first half of the period and watching a film on bullfighting for the second half. Hey, I could deal with that pretty easily. But to my dismay, everybody began to SHOUT, "We don't understand this work and we can't do it!" Remember further back in this book when I told you how students don't like it when a sub knows the subject? That's because they believe that if they say they don't understand the work, they don't have to do it. Well, I knew the subject and they hated me for it immediately. This was one of those times when I did not crack a smile, and turned into a mean looking sourpuss.

To begin with, getting them to be quiet was the biggest challenge of the day, and perhaps, of my career as a substitute teacher. Although I have never attended a rock concert, I have some idea as to the intensity of a thunderous audience. Trying to quiet this class was like undertaking the task of getting the attention of a rock concert audience in order to give them an historical background of the arena they were in. To this day I can still hear the din of this rampant and insubordinate group of not-so charming teenagers.

The Vice-Principal happened to be passing my room at that moment and came in to find out what was going on. I told him I was unable to quiet them down, and asked him for his assistance (which I had never done before) in performing this miraculous feat. It made me feel a little better when even he was unable to get their undivided attention. He admonished the class about their behavior, but the minute he left the room, the roar returned as if never a word of warning had been spoken. They took him as seriously as they took me. That class would not have feared or heeded Atilla the Hun!

This was indeed the class from hell! One girl began to yell, "I need to go to the bathroom." When I announced there would be no hall passes that period, another girl chastised me by telling me I had to let her friend (the potty princess) go.

Let me explain something about bathroom passes. One would assume they are used to go to the bathroom, right? Wrong! Kids seldom ask to use the lavatory because they really need to go. It's hard to determine which request is sincere and which is just an excuse to get out of class and walk around for a few minutes hoping to run into a friend. It's a judgement call for which you develop an intuition. It gets easier after the millionth or so potty request. My feeling that period, was to not let anyone out since it was the last period of the day, and some students may have chosen not to come back.

Actually the idea of some of them not returning was quite appealing. But if a child skips out of school with your knowledge and something happens to him during the school hour, your butt and that of the school systems' are the line. (Imagine a big lawsuit, and you'll suddenly realize how you're dying for that unlikable student to remain in your class.)

At any rate, the class kept chanting, "Let the potty princess go!" I held my ground and refused to give the girl a pass. When this tactic didn't work, the potty princess moved on to another form of harassment and insisted that I turn off the lights while the class was watching a film. When I would not comply with her wish, she began to complain that she was claustrophobic and needed to keep the door open. All I needed was for the whole school to hear that I was unable to keep this class under control. My reputation was on the line here. Although I consistently refused to heed her wishes, this little charmer with bright red lips would get up and open the door anyway. I would close it, and she would open it. Isn't that the kind of games children play with their siblings and not their teachers?

If corporal punishment were legal, performing rhinoplasty on any of those kids without the use of anesthesia would have given me great pleasure. However I knew this was impossible, because a couple of years prior to this incident, a teacher was fired for tweaking a student's nose.

I did not cry, nor did I lunge at anyone physically. But the dark side of my personality (we all have a dark side) began to emerge and my thoughts were, "to kill or not to kill." Although I prudently chose "not to kill," I let out a loud shriek and simultaneously banged on the desk so hard that for at least ten seconds everyone became quiet. I then began to chide the little pain in the butt, by informing her that in my entire career of teaching, she was by far the most disrespectful and the most obnoxious child I had ever had the displeasure of dealing with. This was one of those rare times when I went totally ballistic. (I'm sure it gave the class a lot of pleasure.)

Would you believe, dear readers, that when the class finally ended, (and those forty-five minutes were the longest forty-five minutes of my life) that nasty child complained that I had hurt her feelings and asked me how I dared to have the audacity to berate her in front of her friends? The sad part is, she wasn't kidding because she told me she didn't see anything wrong with her conduct. My analysis of this behavior was to blame either her hormones or her upbringing. I came to the conclusion it was probably a combination of both.

I never substituted for that class again that year. First of all, the teacher didn't ask me again because a friend of mine at school who wanted to kill that child on my behalf told the teacher about my problems with her class. Second, I would not have tackled that class a second time for all the money in the world. Their teacher had my sincerest condolences, and I began to question my sanity every time I subbed for a class that had any of those students in it.

Although that year was probably the most insufferable time of my teaching career as a substitute teacher, I did not quit that day nor that year despite the fact I frequently encountered all of those little darlings in other classes. That's because I am resilient and a survivor, (someone had to survive to be able to write about all this) and also because in my heart I will always have a great deal of faith in youngsters. However, I could never look the little big-mouthed brat in the eye again. The behavior and attitude of that entire ninth grade class continued to be a source of annoyance throughout their four years of high school. One would like to believe that most of them matured somewhat by the time they were seniors. *Aux contraire!* Some teachers who attended their commencement told me, that they were by far the rowdiest and most uncontrolled group ever to graduate from that school. Good luck, World, you have something to look forward to!

Thinking back, I have often wondered what was in the stars the year all those children were conceived, and I have come to the conclusion that perhaps the Chinese Zodiac included The Year of the Werewolf!!! That must be it! That was the same year I also discovered that I too must be slightly masochistic. But that was then and this is now and so, my theme songs are, "The Party's Over" because "I Haven't Got Time For the Pain."

Chapter Eight

Deception

There are several aspects of deception performed by children of all ages. I use the word perform because the way they go about attempting to deceive teachers is a performance to behold. These forms of deception include lying, forgery, cutting classes and cheating. Just because I know kids can be deceptive does not mean I dislike them. It simply means that through experience I have learned to sharpen my skills for catching kids trying to put one over on the teacher. Perhaps what I share with you will make you more aware of what they are capable of pulling.

Lying

The TV program "20/20" did a segment on lying, focusing on very young children. The main reason given for their lying was to keep them out of trouble. I guess it's true that being too honest can get you into trouble. However it went on to show how much of children's lying is learned by observing and emulating their parents. Who else can they blame? Not the media or the government or the school staff. No, we parents are always to blame.

Studies show that lying is partly innate and partly learned. But regardless of the reasons, lying is a fact of life we all must deal with and I think it's safe to say that small white lies are generally harmless. It's when the lies are used to enhance deception that they become unacceptable.

Each generation of kids probably thinks they're the first to come up with such lies as, "I don't have my homework paper because the dog ate it." "I was too sick to do it and here's a note from my parents to prove it." "My grandparents are visiting from China." Or, "I lost my paper with the assignment on it and there was no one I could call to give it to me." Other common lies are, "I'm late for school because I wasn't feeling well this morning," or "my alarm clock didn't go off and my parents overslept also." These falsehoods are usually accompanied by notes from parents verifying them. Now can you see why the blame "lies" on the parents? Come on, didn't you parents all lie at some time or another to prevent your precious children from getting into trouble? Sure you did!

Then we have the not-so-common lies that are actually encouraged by adults. "I'm living with my grandmother in this neighborhood so I can play football for this school" a student once told me. That's one of those logistical tricks that may help the school win football games but teaches the wrong lesson to the student. The football coach said the school principal didn't care because they just wanted a winning team. The parents just let it happen, in hope that their son might win a football scholarship. The student, no doubt, learned warped values. He's an adult now who is probably going through life lying in order to get ahead in this world.

Realistically, lying cannot not be totally eradicated or prevented, but children must also be warned early in life that if they are caught in a lie, they have to pay the consequences.

As I've mentioned, many lies are harmless. It's when the children look me in the eye and swear they're telling the truth (when I know they're not) that I become angry. My personal philosophy is that the consequences for admitting a wrongdoing be less harsh than for lying and not owning up to the mistake. That's what I taught my kids. And despite that rule, I still suspect they lied to me occasionally. I'm sure they felt it was for my own good that I not know certain things. They have always been very protective of me when it behooved them.

A student lying blatantly to teachers or anyone else is unacceptable. Just as a judge in traffic court has heard every excuse under the sun for exceeding the speed limit, teachers have heard every excuse for not having done the homework or for not being prepared for a test. Students also lie about turning in papers, when in fact they did not. Or they swear the flying missiles soaring across the room and hitting me were not thrown by them, but by an unidentified alien whom I failed to see. What I did see was the person who threw it and swore he did not.

Of course there are always legitimate alibis. But a teacher hears them so often, she becomes numbed by them, in turn making the students angry when they are not believed.

Unfortunately, for some people, including the teacher who lied to me, prevarication is a way of life and a problem we as educators and parents should try to correct.

Forgery

One day when I asked Bobby why he didn't have his homework, he handed me a note that said, "Dear Mrs. Mehr, Bobby was too sick to do his homework. Signed, Bobby's mom."

Of course, most kids are smart enough to sign their mother's (or father's) actual name. Some of them get pretty good at it; you can't always tell if it is a forgery.

Most often, children learn to forge their parent's signature before anyone else's, because they have easy access to it. Instead of doing homework, they might spend all evening practicing forgery in order to get out of doing their assignment.

After they've become proficient enough with their parents' name, my guess is they move on and learn to forge teachers' signatures. They figure they can fool the sub because he or she is probably not familiar with the teacher's real signature, or the forgery may just be very authentic looking. In any case, don't believe it if you get a note from the "teacher" saying "Please let the kids play all period" or something like that.

I do believe forged notes did not deceive me too often because when a signature didn't look kosher to me, I would get out my Sherlock Holmes' magnifying glass and investigate the matter by checking with the person whose name was on the note. I just loved playing "gotcha" with the students.

There was an incident involving two girls who cut my class to roam the halls together. (They must have thought they were on the range with buffalo!) A teacher whom I was friends with stopped them and checked to see whether or not they had a pass. They did indeed—with a poor forgery of my initials. My friend reported them to me and I reported them to the Vice-Principal who gave them a two-day suspension. Gotcha, gotcha!!! Two for the price of one. I always love a bargain.

The irony of it all was that they swore to the teacher who stopped them that I had sent them down to their guidance counselors when in fact they had not even showed up to class. Still, I felt insulted that they preferred to roam the halls rather than come to my class. They must have forgotten how much fun I was and how smart I am. It was certainly their loss, not mine.

That incident was amateurish compared to the one involving a boy who consistently cut my class. I might have taken all those cuts personally if I had a tendency for paranoia. (Hey, doesn't anybody like me?) Sunny, the hall monitor caught him and personally ushered him back to the room. The boy displayed a "hall pass" with my signature, which, I must admit, could fool even me. But I knew I hadn't given him the note and therefore assumed he must have traced my unique initials. After he got settled and ready to stay, I asked him how he got a copy of my signature. He proudly admitted he forged it and I can honestly say he did a darn good job of it too. I suspect that this quiet youngster, who was notorious in school for being involved in other unlawful acts, had quite a future ahead of him. I hope I'm wrong.

Cheating

You have all heard the term "stuff happens." (I've cleaned it up a bit because I would like this book to have a "G" rating.) Well my friends, cheating happens. In a survey taken at a high school, 94 percent of the students admitted to having cheated. The other 6 percent probably lied. We may never know. In any case, the statistics are overwhelming and revealing, validating that cheating happens.

With cheating, as with almost everything else, there are degrees. PhDs, MBAs,—hey, I'm joking, but that's really not so far off. By ascending order of severity, the three types of student cheating are copying homework papers, cheating on quizzes, and cheating on tests.

Copying homework is the least severe because the homework is usually not graded, also because the copier may actually learn something (like the osmosis effect)—as long as the copied work is correct. (If it's not, the copier may learn not to cheat.) Admittedly, I remember copying the Latin homework in ninth grade from my friend Stanley who has remained my friend ever since. (Conclusion: copying homework has a bonding effect.) I'm not sure if the person who allowed his or her paper to be copied from is considered a cheater as well. I'll leave that issue up to the moralists to argue over.

In the survey I mentioned, cheating seems to be more prevalent in the eleventh and twelfth grades because of the urgency for higher grades for college admissions. Or, perhaps it is that ninth and tenth graders are more naive and cautious. Frankly, I don't have the answer. I do know that younger children cheat, but with what measure of frequency is the question. Besides, if they lie, then who's to say they don't cheat?

Some school systems give failing grades to students caught cheating on tests. Others suspend cheaters; the United States Naval Academy expels them.

Many teachers schedule tests for times when they know they

are going to be absent, and leave it to the substitutes to deal with cheaters. So often I've had teachers leave an addendum to the lesson plans to make sure I watched out for cheaters. Personally, I always found test days to be pleasant because the students were kept busy the entire period, which resulted in a peaceful session. Of course you need to be constantly alert and on your toes. Proctoring tests is okay as long as your cheating detector is working, (insert batteries before operating) and you use the eyes in back of your head. In the chapter on rules, I forgot to mention that equipment.

Prior to handing out exams, I prefaced the start of the period with "I don't want to see any wandering eyeballs, and if I catch anyone cheating that person will get a zero."

In most cases the class took me seriously. Those who did not learned quickly that I was a woman of my word. (Be consistent and follow through on threats and promises.) However, even with warnings and the "evil eye" look, there were invariably students who thought they could get away with cheating because, "cheating happens." Knowing this, teachers often prepare two sets of test papers; one row gets set A, and the next row gets set B, and so on.

My first memorable experience with cheaters took place in an English class. The teacher for whom I was subbing, Mr. Grammar, was extremely methodical in the way he ran his classroom. He was tough, yet lovable. He kept close track of his tests by numbering each one. Actually, he kept a close eye on everything.

I was naive about giving tests then, and this came at a time when I had just branched out from Music to other subjects. (Actually, English I could handle since it is my primary language.) Anyway, at the beginning of one of the class periods, a large twelfth grade boy told me he would not be taking the test because he had been out of school all week due to an illness. It sounded legitimate to me and so I said okay. I then took attendance and passed out the test papers, inadvertently giving one to the boy who said he wouldn't be taking the exam.

When the class ended, I sorted out the tests and rearranged them in numerical order. To my consternation, I discovered one was missing. I was so disturbed, that twelve years later, I remember it was test #27. (It's my short-term memory that's bad.) I couldn't believe that anyone could do this to me. I took this incident very personally. This came at a time when I was attempting to build up my reputation at the school as being reliable and formidable. (And, I was trying my darndest not to be the archetypal sub.)

I left a note for the teacher informing him of the problem. Somehow I anticipated that he wasn't going to be too thrilled. My suspicions were accurate, because he called me the following night not sounding like a happy camper. He was more than slightly annoyed, not at me so much as the situation I was put into. Although I didn't know many of the students' names at that time, I was able to recall the boy's name that I suspected pulled that fast one. Mr. Grammar agreed with my assumption of who the culprit was, and went after him with a vengeance. Most of his students were smart enough not to fool with him, but thought they could get away with the scheme when a sub was in.

Somehow, Mr. Grammar got the offender to fess up to the crime and I was not looking so bad since I could identify the perpetrator. After that, I got called back to substitute for him many times over the years.

Another time when I was in for the same teacher, another cheating episode occurred involving a spelling test. I went through my usual spiel about the eyeballs and the zeroes and then passed out the tests. I had spent several days with this class, so I got to know everyone by name. Habitually, I would walk up and down the aisles (much like a prison warden) to let the class know I was watching them.

In the middle of the test, one boy who always wore his baseball cap suddenly felt the urge to take it off and put it on top of his desk. I smelled a rat. (Or was it the perspiration of his cap?) Before I even pounced on him, I saw another boy eyeballing his notebook, which was lying on the floor next to him. When I approached the cap, I grabbed it like a hungry vulture and found the spelling list attached to the inside of the visor. With my other claw, I swooped up the notebook from the floor and guess what I found there? Another spelling list! Two for the price of one, how I love those "two-fers!"

I mortified these two boys simultaneously. They were totally taken aback by my sharp sense of perception. (Those batteries never stopped working.) Every time they saw me after that incident, the one boy would say, "Mrs. Mehr, I can't believe you caught us cheating." The other swore he didn't cheat. He claimed he only kept that list close by "just in case." That is, just in case I wasn't watching and he needed to check a spelling or definition. He also swore up and down that he never used the list, so in essence that was not real cheating.

Both boys begged and pleaded with me to ignore their cheating. But I told them in no uncertain terms that couldn't I do that, since it would make me an accomplice, and I wouldn't be doing my job honestly. I gave both boys zeroes for the test, and the teacher called their parents to inform them of what transpired. They got a double whammy for their dishonesty.

The most obvious and tell-tale ways to detect potential cheaters are to watch those students while taking an exam who keep looking up to see if the teacher is watching them. When I saw that happening, I would walk the aisles and position myself near the student who looked suspicious. Or, I would stand in back of the room so the students couldn't tell if they were being watched. Most kids are so busy doing their own work, they have no time to look up and check the whereabouts of the teacher. It's the ones who don't know the material, that look around the room a lot. I often thought they were looking for some guardian angel to give them the answers.

Another unforgettable experience was the time I gave a final exam in calculus. I know as much about calculus as I know about astrophysics, which is zero. But, I do know how to ad-lib and administer tests.

At any rate, all I had to do was hand out papers, proctor the students, collect their papers and leave them in the teacher's mailbox. (I meant leave the papers, not the students, in the teacher's mailbox, although the latter sometimes seemed like a good idea.)

Things were going smoothly until the end of one of the class periods. One boy approached me after I had collected all the completed papers and asked me if he could have his paper back because after he turned it in, he realized he had made a mistake and wanted to change an answer. But I had already seen him check his textbook and I replied, "that request is denied." It was heartbreaking to see the boy beg, and disconcerting to hear him claim his request was not unreasonable, especially when he kept reiterating that if he did not do well on the test he would not be admitted to the college of his choice. He made it sound as though his whole future depended on one answer.

For just a few seconds I was overwhelmed with a feeling of power. By helping him cheat I would be able to control his future. Of course I refused his plea and asked him if his teacher had been there would he still have made the same request, and would his teacher ever agree to let him change his answer. "No, but that's because Mr. K is not a nice guy," he said. "I guess I'm not such a nice guy either," I quipped.

This boy was relentless. He followed me to the lunchroom. He waited for me after school and pleaded with me. But I didn't give in. He then accused me of being the one who would prevent him from getting into college. That's funny, because I didn't realize that the academic achievements one established during four years of high school was meaningless. And I also didn't realize it hinged on how one did in a calculus final. He seemed to feel that if I didn't help him cheat, his life wasn't worth living.

Since it was the end of the school year, I never got around to asking the calculus teacher how this boy made out or even discussed with him what had transpired. So, to this day I still lose sleep over this boy's future (Not). And, I wonder too, that if in fact he got into the college of his choice, did he beg the professors to let him change an answer on a test? Who knows, stranger things have happened.

Then there was the time I caught a boy with the answers to his final chemistry exam printed on a piece of paper so small you practically needed a magnifying glass to read it. It must be an art form to be able to print that small and be able to read it while cheating on an exam. (Perhaps the teacher who had written his lesson plans so small had mastered that art form as a student himself.) I wrote a little tiny zero on the exam; it had a great effect on his final grade.

I just realized that my stories seem somewhat biased. The cheaters I have spoken of were all of the male persuasion. In my experiences, the most blatant cheaters have been boys. Perhaps some of you have encountered more girls cheating, but for me, that was not the case.

For those of you who have not spent any time teaching in a classroom, you are probably shocked at the frequency with which cheating occurs. Teachers need eyes in back of their heads. But if they had them, I guess they wouldn't be in a classroom—they'd be in a circus instead. So let's go with what we've got.

I saved the best story for last. A young entrepreneur, who began his own business at age twelve, had several of his friends mow lawns while he collected a part of the revenue. From the way I remember it, he went on to other types of businesses using kids his age. The community was so proud of him, his story got written up in the local newspapers. And, he was making so much money, he was able to employ a chauffeur to drive him around because he was not old enough to drive.

I don't remember all the specifics of his techniques, (If I did, I might be riding around with a chauffeur myself.) but I do know he became notorious. By the time this young mogul reached high school age he was (in his mind) too sophisticated to mingle with the rest of the peons and attend classes on a regular basis. When he was old enough to buy his own car, he obtained a handicap sticker and blatantly parked in a handicap space. Everyone knew he was not handicapped, (unless he had a golfers handicap) but he was nevertheless able to get away with it because school security investigated and found the sticker to be valid. (I wonder whom he paid off for that one.) Seeing him get out of his car and cockily swagger into school infuriated the faculty, and probably gave him much joy.

Teachers were not thrilled with this whiz kid. First of all, he rarely attended classes. Second, when he did attend, he usually aced tests although he didn't seem particularly brilliant when he was in class. The little stinkweed always ended up smelling like a flower. That is, until he became a senior and was nearly about to graduate. As you all know, seniors take the SAT exam in order to get into college. That is, most seniors.

Mr. Mogul did so well on his SAT scores, he managed to get a scholarship to a small college. Everything seemed to be going right for him until someone overheard him bragging about how he managed to get such high scores on the SAT exam. Apparently, anonymous phone calls were made to the SAT Board, and after careful investigation, two cheaters were exposed.

The story goes, he paid a very bright college student to take the exam for him. Apparently, he was able to obtain an illegal identification for his friend who was caught and ended up suffering the consequences as well. It was one of the biggest scandals our community ever experienced, and the story was reported nationwide.

He might have gotten away with cheating if he hadn't bragged. But con artists need to feel important and therefore, he needed to show how he could outsmart the world. At that point, Mr. Ex-entrepreneur was not allowed to attend college and was convicted of fraud by the SAT Board. He ended up serving time in jail for the offense, and the friend who took the test for him was expelled from the prestigious university he was attending.

This was not your ordinary cheater story. However, it was the epitome of cheating. In all probability, most cheaters don't end up as felons. It might be interesting to conduct a survey where one could question convicted swindlers and find out if they cheated on school exams.

In case I haven't cited all the ways one can cheat, I've compiled a list, which you might be able to refer to when you administer a test.

(1). Looking at someone else's paper.

(2). Asking (quietly) for an answer from a classmate.

(3). Writing the answers on the hand, the arm, the leg, the bottom of the shoe, the visor of a cap, etc.

(4). Sitting in back of someone who will place his pencil (if it's a multiple choice exam) on the top left hand corner of his desk if the answer is A, the top right hand corner if the answer is B, etc.

(5). Putting the answers under the test paper and hoping the teacher won't catch you looking at them (unless she's blind).

(6). Sitting next to a window and taping the answers to it so you and others with Superman's xray vision can see them as well.

(7). Asking students who already took the test earlier, what the questions are.

There is one more that I credit myself for uncovering, which is by far the newest and most unique form of cheating. (When I made the discovery, I felt like Christopher Columbus discovering the Americas.) In the last few years, sophisticated graphing calculators are being used in the science and math classes, and students are often permitted to use them during testing sessions. However, answers can also be stored in the calculators. Evidently, the kids would store the answers in them and pass them along to their friends in other classes. They were getting away with this until one day, a boy told me he was unable to make up the exam, which the teacher left for him. I said it was all right with me and that I would let his teacher know. After a couple of minutes, I observed a quick exchange of calculators, and the student suddenly decided he was ready to take the exam. Watching this boy write down his answers so fast and so furiously made my cheating detector go off, triggering my suspicious antenna which shot up like a periscope in a submarine. With that, I walked over to him with another calculator and said, "Use this one instead." As suddenly as he decided to take the test, that's how suddenly he decided not to take it. Gotcha! I passed this information along to the department heads and to the teachers, who ultimately had to make sure all the calculators were cleared before test time. This is just one more unnecessary nuisance teachers need to deal with, and these are the types of nonsensical interruptions that take away valuable teaching time.

Unfortunately, there is no Utopia, and we all must deal with the realities of life. Oh, to live in Shangri-La!

The following methods of cheating were given to me by some students (unsigned) when I requested suggestions from them for material for this book.

(1). Shove the test and textbook down your pants and ask to go to the bathroom. Finish the test in the bathroom.

(2). Etch the answers on your fingernails.

(3). On a multiple-choice exam, devise a code with your pencil.

(4). Write the answers on the insides of your eyelids. To see them, close your eyes and look straight at a light bulb. This might cause health problems if used frequently.

The possibilities are endless, and of course the irony of it all is that the time that is wasted devising devious methods could be well spent learning the material and taking a test without having to cheat.

Chapter Nine

Harassment

Just as hurricanes and tornadoes are natural phenomena, harassment toward substitute teachers is also a natural occurrence. Students of all ages do it both wittingly and unwittingly to vent their frustrations, much of which may have to do with their regular teacher. When they see a sub walk in, they instinctively know their chances of getting away with "acting up" or, to use today's psychophraseology, "acting out" are pretty good.

Although students' harassment may come across as an act to undermine your authority, keep in mind that to them it is releasing the tension of the everyday rigors of home, school, and classroom. It is comic relief at your expense, but you'll make it worse by not having a sense of humor. You might as well take it lightly (except when it's truly serious) because it's practically in the job description. According to my standards, if a class was generally well behaved and not out of control, my manner was light, yet strict. I got to be a stand-up comedienne like Mrs. Davis (a sub) had told me I should be when I was a kid. You see, harassment of subs is a generational cycle, and that's another reason why you shouldn't lose your cool—unless you can honestly say that you never harassed a sub when you were a kid.

Anyway, when the mood lent itself to good-natured bantering, my rule as a stand-up sub was that no one was allowed to be funny except me. Just kidding! I enjoyed students' nonmalicious joking. When they crossed the line into malice, that's what I considered harassment and that's when I put my foot down. Not on students' heads, although I felt like it sometimes. I felt like mashing that boy who pursued me all day trying to get me to change an answer on his final exam. Also, that girl who hounded me about closing a door, and kept turning off the lights to watch a movie and harassing me about not letting her friend go to the bathroom. Perhaps you remember those two from earlier chapters. I'll never forget them.

There was a difference in the form of harassment by male and female students. The girls who didn't like me, (hard for me to understand, because to know me is to love me) were sassy and would either give me dirty looks when I reprimanded them or they would comment about my having a bad day or that I didn't like them. (No, I was not PMS-ing.) My standard answer was, "I love you all, and I was not in a bad mood until some of you showed up in class today."

The worst harassment I ever got took place in an art history class. It was a three-day assignment, and one of the days included showing a video. (What else?) One particular class had two clowns in it who always gave me a hard time. I'll call them Mutt and Jeff because of the differences in their height.

Even when Mutt and Jeff were separated, they were a thorn in my (back) side no matter what class they were in. Mutt was the kind of guy who when I was his sub in gym, would tease the other students by throwing basketballs at them or, somehow, manage to cover a large part of the gym floor with gum wrappers. What amazed me was how he was able to get a hold of so many wrappers.

For those offenses, I turned Mutt in to the Vice-Principal who warned him that if this type of behavior persisted, his parents would be contacted and brought in for a conference. I was there while the admonishment took place, and I wish I had a camera with me to capture the look of remorse on Mutt's face. He was another sure Oscar-winner. He promised faithfully that he would never throw basketballs at students again. Well, he may have kept that promise, but he continued to annoy me in other ways.

Jeff, on the other hand, never did anything that was physically abusive to other students. He was just a kind of noodge, the sort of kid who would constantly show up late for class or fail to return to class after a split lunch. (Kids did this often when they had a sub.)

Together in that class, Mutt and Jeff were worse than Beavis and Butthead. They walked around the room annoying the other students and disrupting those who were working. When I told them to go back to their seats and do their work, they claimed they had already finished their project. If I believed that, they had some land on Uranus they could sell me as well.

(Get it, your anus? I wish I had a dollar for every time a kid used that one, thinking it was original. I'd be a billionaire. Okay, only a millionaire.)

Anyway, day two (who's counting?) I was to show the video. Although I had promised myself, ever since the porno flick incident, that I would never leave the machine unguarded, I forgot, and walked away from it for a reason that slips my mind. Luckily, this time I turned—I caught Jeff in the act, caught him red-handed, and he knew it. I beat him to the video machine and took the tape out. "Gimme that tape," Jeff said. "It's mine." I refused. "That's a project we're working on," said Mutt. He and Jeff surrounded me and moved threateningly close.

"If it's a school project," I said, "perhaps the Vice Principal would find it interesting. Would you guys mind if I showed it to him?" Jeff grabbed my arm to force the tape out of my hand. This was now beyond harassment; it was physical abuse. However, these particular boys, I knew, were not really dangerous—they were clowns, not criminals. I ordered them to report to the Vice-Principal's office.

At the end of the day, I had a conference with the Vice-Principal and gave him my version of the incident. He decided Mutt and Jeff would report to his office the next day instead of coming to my class. The following day there was a school assembly which most of the students attended. Those who did not choose to attend could stay in the classroom and do work. Only two did, so things were pretty quiet.

Just as I was enjoying the calm, Mutt and Jeff suddenly turned up at the door. "The veep said we could come to class if we were good," one or the other of them said. "Go back to the office!" I shouted. They began to call me names and make obscene gestures. I ran to the door to escort them personally to the office. They eluded me and ran away yelling like a couple of hyenas. I was so angry, I ran after them and when I could not find them I marched to the office. The Vice-Principal was at the assembly and would return at its conclusion. "What's wrong?" the secretary asked. I know my face was beet-red with fury. When I told her the problem, she summoned the hall monitors who found the gruesome twosome and escorted them to the office.

Later that day, I had another tete-a-tete with the VP to inform him that stronger measures needed to be taken regarding the abusive behavior I had sustained. We decided I would write a letter to him, which he would forward to the parents informing them of their children's abusive behavior. I never had to put up with Mutt or Jeff again, because anytime I subbed for any of their classes, they were to report to the VP's office.

I tell you: I've been harassed—and I've been HARASSED. This next incident involved an eleventh grade boy who from the first time he laid eyes on me began to tell me how much he loved me. (I told you to know me is to love me.) Somehow, I don't remember ever having him in my classes while he was in ninth and tenth grade. This kid walked into my class with a grin on his face that resembled that of a Cheshire cat. He was certainly pleasant enough. He introduced himself to me and shook my hand.

You might be thinking it was a polite gesture. Maybe so, but it had been my experience with students, that those who let me know who they were the first time they saw me usually had a past. Most students, when they first saw me, an unfamiliar sub, would just walk past me with a blank look on their faces. The ones who identified themselves were the ones whose names I would have learned without their introduction.

This young man, I soon learned, was not a troublemaker, but simply a lazy student who suffered from romantic delusions. After I took attendance and wrote the (Spanish) assignment on the board, this Don Juan pulled his chair up and sat backward, hunched over the backboard, spread-legged. "Let's chat," he said. "I'm not here to socialize," I said. "Do your assignment." I'm no good in Spanish," he answered. (His teacher later confirmed that.)

He persisted in asking me inane questions, and said, "I love you, you are my princess." "I would love you to do your assignment and leave me alone," I said. He grinned, and seemed to enjoy my sarcasm.

From that time on whenever this Don Juan was in my class, he would insist on making conversation instead of completing his assignment. Mr. Juan, who believed he was quite the ladies man, began to hug me every time he saw me. Mind you, sexual harassment by teachers was a hot issue at the time, so I had to be careful not to do anything that could be taken as an affectionate gesture. I politely informed him this was unacceptable behavior and said "If you touch me again, I will report you to the Vice-Principal."

A summer passed, and somehow Don Juan-a bee made it into the 12th grade. I tried to avoid him, but one day in the halls, he grabbed me and kissed me on the lips. I didn't say anything to him, but simply marched myself down to the Vice-Principal's office (again) and told him about Don Juan-a bee. "He's intolerable," I said. "He's just trying to be cute," said the veep. But he agreed that kind of behavior was not to be tolerated and said he would speak to Don about it.

Obviously my admonishments had no affect on Don, but a word from an administrator did the job, because the next time I saw him, he just walked on by and gave me a coy smile. I did not find Don's behavior cute. Cute was when a senior boy in a previous year used to call me, "his woman." He never got touchy feely with me and he was a good student as well.

Evidently, Don's friends knew about his behavior and found out I had turned him in. One of them informed me, after exchanging a "high five," that he had been warned by some of his friends that eventually a teacher would turn him in for being a "kissing bandit." I presume he was doing it to other female teachers as well. From that time on, there was a comfortable distance between us and conversation was kept to a minimum.

There is no doubt in my mind that most experienced educators have endured some form of harassment, some perhaps more serious than others. Therefore what I've imparted to you might not be revolutionary but just examples for those not familiar with the trials and tribulations occurring within the walls of our educational system. History repeats itself over and over again. Remember what Socrates said about youth in his era? He said, "Children today are tyrants. They contradict their parents, gobble their food and tyrannize their teachers". So it goes with every ensuing generation of youth. And most have survived.

Perhaps I'm a little overly suspicious, but I do believe substitutes are harassed more than regular teachers. Every teacher in every school system should impart to their students that subs are to get the same respect they give to their teachers, and that administrators support them as did the administrators with whom I dealt.

The message should be made loud and clear to the troublemakers, alerting them to the fact that the same disciplinary action used for misconduct toward teachers will be equally enforced for offenses toward substitutes.

A word of warning: If you even suspect there might be a potential danger to your well-being or to the well-being of other students, do not be a hero (not the SUB sandwich) or a martyr. Send for HELP!

Chapter Ten

Children With Special Needs

A serious and sensitive issue that needs closer scrutiny and modification is the lack of information rendered to substitutes in regard to children with special needs. Every school has a confidential file on these students.

And for all I know, they may even have one on subs and teachers. If they do, I know at least one sub whose file should say, "is afflicted with bouts of PMS—Permanent Menstrual Syndrome," and another's "suffers from prostate incontinence." There is also a principal I know who has such a large ego, he cannot fit through the front door, who immodestly admitted to a member of his staff that he was one of the system's best-looking, best-dressed and most ambitious principal that he knew, and would survive the longest in the school system. Now *that* is a large ego if I've ever seen one. Should there be a file on him?

All kidding aside, the focus of this chapter (I'll try to stay focused) is the omission of information to subs, in the service of maintaining confidentiality concerning children with special needs.

Confidential files are reserved for use by administrators, teachers, and counselors which I agree is justifiable. Certainly, the professional who is dealing with such a student should be prepared for any potential problems. Therefore, I suggest that any vital information which a teacher has access to, be passed along to the unsuspecting substitutes since emergencies arise more often than one may expect.

(Have you noticed how the phrase, "unsuspecting substitutes" keeps recurring? That's because so frequently, subs often start the day, fat dumb and happy, unaware of what may be in store for them, hoping to face a group of precious, loving students who are just thrilled to see a sub, and eager to get their work done. If you believe that fantasy, you are probably delusional and living in La La Land.)

In any given school, there are going to be children, just like us adults, with medical problems, psychological problems, physical disabilities or family crises. But, even though these issues are serious, there were unexpected situations that arose (and nearly caused me to have apoplexy) which in retrospect seem funny to me. They may not appear funny to others, but I suppose it's because each of us perceives a given situation quite differently. (Although at times I seem to possess a warped sense of humor, I am in fact a sensitive person who does not find an individual's affliction a laughing matter.)

I think it's a good idea for a sub to ask that a teacher provide, along with lesson plans, rosters and seating charts, a brief description of a student's special needs. (That is, if the teacher dutifully leaves a folder.) Every teacher who has a coded* student, (*Having a special problem.) has the data on hand and should pass it along to subs.

By suggesting that certain confidential information be given to substitutes, I am not implying these personal records be made available to just anyone—subs are not just anyone. Nor should they be published in the local newspapers for public consumption. Everyone is entitled to privacy. I'm simply emphasizing that subs must be considered professionals and be informed of a child's need, as are the other professionals who must deal with the problems. It's fair to us and to the students as well.

There may be students who are on medication, who routinely go to the health room to take them. Some require prescription drugs while others may occasionally need over-the-counter drugs. Not having been informed of a student needing to legitimately leave the class, a sub might become suspicious and assume the student is looking for an excuse to roam the halls. (Not unusual.) Other students at times may go to other teachers for special help or even to a different room to take a test because extra time is needed. These are all fine reasons for leaving the room. But my acquired suspicious nature often led me to believe the students were trying to pull a fast one, in which case I would double check to see they were in fact permitted to leave class, and whether they showed up at their designated destination without making detours. This is why it is desirable for a sub to know about the various changes with which regular teachers are already familiar.

In regard to medications, please give me some latitude to expound for a moment. (Actually, I've become such a rebel, that even if you don't allow me to expound, I'm going to anyway. Subbing did that to me.)

Presently, taking medications in school can be a complicated issue. Students, who ingest pills unmonitored, can be suspended. With regard to all the new rulings on drugs and their uses and abuses, a teacher or sub must observe extreme caution in aiding a girl suffering from menstrual pains by allowing her to take Midol or aspirin without going to the health room. In most school systems, a teacher is not allowed to give a student anything that is considered a drug. Naturally, it is for her own protection. But these days, innocent children get suspended because they are unaware of the consequences of unwittingly taking medications like Midol or aspirin without supervision, and they don't have the excuse of being a dumb jock.

(Give me a break, world! Isn't it ludicrous how our society in many instances forgives and overlooks drug and alcohol abuse by certain prestigious student athletes, offenders who should probably be thrown off their team and/or be in rehab, while an honor student gets suspended for taking an over-the-counter drug to relieve cramps? In order to get a point across, measures are carried to the extreme without using sound judgement. What's wrong with taking into account both the source and the circumstance before passing a "guilty" verdict on a naive child and stigmatizing, her for the rest of her school career? It's impossible to have a "one size fits all" rule for the whole world, which is why we have amendments to our Constitution.)

Once upon a time while I was subbing in a foreign language class, a girl fell off her chair onto the floor. (Believe me this is no fairy tale.) She appeared to be having an epileptic seizure. I jumped out of my seat to see what I could do. Only one student in the class reacted; the rest of the class ignored the situation as if it were an everyday occurrence. In fact, I would later learn that it was indeed a seizure, a frequent occurrence for that child. The girl who did respond had been assigned to get the nurse when a seizure occurred. But can you imagine how inept I felt standing there, not knowing what was going on? (Actually not being a paramedic, I couldn't have done much anyway except send for assistance.) A short note from the teacher alerting me of the possibility of a seizure occurring would have been considerate. But you know people aren't always considerate; that's why I make it a point to ask teachers if students have any special needs I should know about. Anyway, the girl regained consciousness within two minutes and assured me she was fine. Still the nurse came and took her to the health room.

On another day when I was in for a gym teacher, I was instructed to have the girls jog around the track five times, instead of the running the usual aerobics exercise video, and that was fine with me. Mind you this was after the porno flick and breaking the VCR connection incidents, so anything to do with videos made me nervous.

When I announced what the activity for the class would be, the girls moaned and groaned as if "five laps" meant running the "Boston Marathon." Laziness is a common affliction amongst many teens. Many adults too, including me—or maybe I'm just a recycled teenager.

My job was not to just stand there and enjoy the fresh air, but to check off each girl's name each time she ran a lap. They would yell out their names when they passed me, while I looked up and down the list of fifty-two names making sure I checked off the right one. During the twenty-minute jogging session, two girls passed out in the middle of the track, which was a good distance from the main office. (Is there such a thing as a bad distance?) My first feeling was that if these girls would have gotten off their lazy teenage butts, they may not have passed out from five measly laps.

Fortunately, another teacher whose class was on the track, attended to the girls while I ran for help. Would you believe the nurse was not there that day? (Where is she when you really need her?)

That meant that one of the beloved secretaries who was very good in a crisis took charge of the situation. She called the paramedics, had someone else contact the parents, and then comforted the girls.

(Not only did she know how to act like a principal, she was also proficient at tending to health emergency problems when the nurse was unavailable. In all honesty, she really was good, and yet so self-assured, that she intimidated even the other secretary, who, when she came to help, nervously asked me if I knew exactly what Secretary NUMBER ONE wanted her to do. I did not. But nevertheless, it's interesting to observe how when you "act" authoritative, people really believe and fear you.)

As you may have guessed, those two girls each had a medical problem of which I was not forewarned. One of the girls was asthmatic, and the other suffered from an esophageal reflux condition. When the ambulance arrived, they were taken to the locker room, which was now off limits to the rest of the girls in the class who had to change back into street clothes. I was instructed to lock the doors and not let anyone in while the paramedics tended to the ill students. Girls from another gym class who didn't know what had happened started banging on the doors and yelling because they wanted to come in and get dressed. Suddenly they were in a hurry. (Most teenagers are never in a hurry unless they are going to lunch, trying to catch a ride home with a friend, or illegally skipping out of school.) The two girls ultimately were taken to the hospital because their parents could not be located. They recovered quickly and were taken home the same day. (Besides, nowadays you almost have to be dying before you're allowed to stay overnight in a hospital!)

Now can you see how emergencies arise during the course of a day? Although it is true that most of us have limited capabilities in administering medical assistance, other than to trying to obtain help as quickly as possible, some forewarning could save valuable time when a sub is made aware of potential problems. These are serious issues that school administrators need to be more aware of.

Then there was the time I almost put my foot in my mouth when I encountered a new ninth grade class, without knowing about a certain boy's illness. An enthusiastic and talkative bunch of students entered my classroom. I had not yet looked up to see them, but what I heard was someone talking like Donald Duck and chattering his head off. I was not planning to say anything unless this continued during class time.

I was about to say, "Hey you, stop clowning around!" until I looked up and saw the trachea tube in his throat. Thank goodness I did look up before I made a sarcastic remark, because I would have felt like a worm if I had not realized he had a health problem. I later found out this child was being treated for throat cancer and unsure of his prognosis. I'd say that was a bigger problem than my initial annoyance at his Donald Duck voice.

There have been other incidents, which were not quite as critical as the ones I have just cited. A couple of them in particular come to mind, which I believe were certainly more amusing, and worth relating.

There was a very timid-looking ninth-grade student, who always carried a laptop computer and used it to do all his work on it, while the other students used textbooks and paper. One day, he apprehensively approached me to ask permission to go to the health room. Couldn't he come up with something more original? (I wish I had a dime for every student who needed to use the bathroom or go to the health room during class time.)

Well, before this frightened-looking child could finish his sentence, he began throwing up in front of me. (Honestly folks, I'm not that scary or intimidating!) I put the wastepaper basket under him while he just stood there vomiting, and told him he did not need a note.

(Vomiting in the halls would surely suffice. I couldn't imagine the hall monitors stopping him while he ran through the halls, puking. Well, I take that back, knowing some of them as I did. I could just picture Sunny the Smiling Monitor saying, "let me see your hall pass" while this pathetic child is standing there trying to explain that he was too sick to wait for one, and that the dumb sub sent him out without it. In which case, if he was stopped, I hope he vomited all over Sunny!)

When I reminisce over some of these moments, I get vindictive and my blood pressure becomes elevated because when certain people are given a bit of authority, they become crazed with it. These tough dudes had on occasion reported me to a higher authority (not the REAL Higher Authority) because I hadn't issued a hall pass, which on my part was for a good reason. But the big guys in the halls felt compelled to report it instead of discussing the infraction with me first.

Their self-importance was even extended to the faculty parking lot where they were stationed every morning to avert students from using it. They felt cocky enough to reprimand teachers for entering the lot the wrong way. Rebel that I am, I would do it anyway, and when I was caught, I was told under no uncertain terms that if I did it again, I would be reported. (I wonder if I would have gotten detention?)

Anyway, the room now smelled like a vomitorium, and the kids were acting all grossed out, exaggeratingly so, saying "ew gross!" and it was actually pretty bad. Some ran out of the room. I began to wonder who was going to clean up? I threw some paper towels over the mess and sent a boy out to get custodial help. Him I gave a note to. (The boy, not the custodian.) I remember thinking the custodians probably appreciated the vomit less than I did. But after all, they've got to make a living.

Soon after that incident, I never saw the timid boy in school again. To this day, I still wonder what his problem was, (besides being sick to his stomach) and what happened to him. He seemed to have vanished into thin air.

Since I'm on the topic of being remiss in regard to issuing hall passes, I'm reminded of the time when I had to send a whole math class to their lockers to get their books because the students did not normally bring them to class, and their teacher had taken off unexpectedly. I permitted them all to leave without hall passes. There are always extenuating circumstances to most regulations. Guess who they ran into? No, not Smilin' Sunny the friendly monitor, but the principal who reprimanded everyone for not having those sacred passes. He relayed a message to me via a student, that I was not to let anyone out of class without a note. Once again he did not tell me face to face. I think that after the other sub sued him, he was hesitant about reprimanding subs in person.

Where was this person's common sense, and how could he possibly expect a teacher to issue thirty-two passes? By the time she finished writing them, the class would be over. Besides, the whole class wouldn't be lying about not having their books. Furthermore, I was not in the habit of letting more than one or two students out at the same time if occasionally someone forgot to bring a book. After a while, we old pros get a feel for legitimate requests.

I apologize for the periodic wild tangents, but the fact is that substituting can do that to you because during the course of a

92 JUDY SAUL MEHR

normal school day there are several distractions, which seem to multiply when a sub is present, including fire drills.

I've got one more puke story I just have to tell you about. I was conducting a junior high school choir in a holiday concert when all of a sudden the choir began to part like the Red Sea. At first I thought Moses reincarnated, but no, this was not happening because of some miracle. The parting occurred because a boy in the back row was puking his guts out. Hallelujah! When I realized what was happening, I motioned for him to go, and my choir, so well trained by *moi*, continued the concert as if nothing was wrong.

I mention this boy because I think, like many youngsters, he was too shy and embarrassed to admit he had a problem, even a minor one like an upset stomach. Most children like to keep a low profile so they don't appear different from their peers. That's just one more thing that makes a sub's job challenging, so it helps to be sensitive to special needs, and be alert and ready when problems arise. And I promise you, they WILL arise.

Chapter Eleven

Substitute Gripes

Although the many gripes I will share with you stem primarily from my own experiences, they reflect most all other substitutes' gripes as well.

By far, the number one gripe is the salary. It is so scanty, that I find it to be a source of embarrassment. Embarrassing for the school systems and embarrassing for the subs who need to work for such little money. I say that, yet I just left the highest paying system in the Washington, D.C. area, which itself is one of the most affluent metropolitan areas in the country. Imagine how it must be for subs in other systems.

Has any school system ever considered what subs are really worth? They certainly have not! (I like answering my own questions because I know I will always come up with the correct answer. I'm sure if school board members answered the question, they would give the opposite response.)

Furthermore, while Montgomery County continuously reiterates that it pays relatively high, the public never hears about the stricter requirements needed to work for this system: a teaching degree or a non-teaching degree with some teaching experience. (How could a non-teacher teach?) Most other systems have no such criteria. They may use people with only a high school degree or two years of college. But that doesn't mean those systems are easier to work for; it just means they're looking for a warm body to fill in for the teacher, and they'll compromise standards rather than pay for quality.

Previously I stated that the school system for which I worked went six years without giving subs a raise. And by the time I finish this book it will probably be even longer. It did give a meager bonus to those who had worked seven hundred hours. (I personally found it demeaning, and by the time they took out taxes, I barely found it at all.) Everyone in the system got a cost of living increase except the subs. Why are we subs being discriminated against? Do I see a lot of hands going up to answer this question? My answer is "we have no representation and no one who really gives a darn, as long as teachers get coverage!" (Hey, subs out there, do you agree with me?)

Bus drivers are making approximately a dollar an hour less than subs, and custodians make more than subs. Maybe I should consider becoming a bus driver. For almost the same pay I would be a lot less stressed. (Can't you just here me singing, "The wheels on the bus go round and round, round and round, round and round?"

Now, do you see the inequities in pay? If you don't, then you're probably on the budget committee of the school board! Although they (I'm not sure who they are either) constantly remind us that we are still the highest paid subs in the area, the bottom line is, that none of us is making what we deserve. We are unequivocally worth our weight in gold!!! If there's anyone out there who disagrees with me, he or she should try being a sub for a couple of days.

For those of you who are unfamiliar as to how subs are paid, I will explain it to you briefly. There are two different pay scales. (No, you don't get to choose from Column A or Column B.) One is short-term pay and the other is long-term pay. (It almost sounds like a prison sentence, and sometimes it even feels like one.) Short-termers receive X amount of dollars per day whether they work twenty days in succession (but not on the same assignment) or one day a week. Long-termers receive about twenty-five to thirty dollars a day more, beginning on the eleventh day of an assignment. In other words, long-termers were getting short-term pay for the first ten days, and then the higher amount beginning on the eleventh day.

They have just changed that policy here so that after the tenth day subs would receive retroactive long-term pay. It must be because they heard about this book and were worried that I would be exposing them. I'd like to believe I have that kind of influence. Anyway, that new ruling is only fair! The long-term sub's duties are nonetheless the same as the teacher she is replacing, and she is getting paid half as much as the regular teacher no matter how much experience the sub has.

Sometimes when there is a hiring freeze, some systems use subs when a position is open in order to spend less money, and of course, the same high quality of teaching is expected. What is seriously wrong with all this is that subs are not being paid for emergency days when they cannot work. If they miss more than three days in a row, they are kicked back to the daily rate of pay until they work ten days again. Are you confused yet? If not, I at least hope you're infuriated. The bottom line to this is total inequity for sub pay. The DOLLARS and SENSE don't add up to the work that is expected to be accomplished. I suppose this expectation carries over to any temporary position because most temp jobs never pay well. That includes lawyers who when on temporary assignments will make, perhaps between ten and fifteen dollars per hour while full-time permanent attorneys make one hundred dollars and up per hour.

Because of a lack of uniformity, many subs have expressed the need for a guidebook from their system describing and delineating the duties of the subs as well as listing opening and closing times for schools. In many systems, elementary, middle schools, and high schools open at different times.

Suppose you are an art teacher and you can sub from grades K-12, (don't forget the finger-painting bit), and the computer does not give you the times. How are you supposed to find it out? From what I've been told computers don't always give you that information. In which case I guess you just show up to school whenever. Of course I'm being facetious, but I've also been made aware of the fact that at times the computer does not give you the grade or the specific subject matter you have been requested to sub for. If you are subbing at a high school, the computer might tell you that the job is in the science department, but will not specifically name whether it is lab science or chemistry. It's nice to have that information ahead of time because we subs have a natural curiosity for such details.

If the system is a large one, then it has been suggested that each school has the secretary prepare a guide, outlining what the principal expects of the sub, and include a list of the faculty's names along with what they teach and a master schedule. I'm sure the secretary will be thrilled to do this. Not only should the principals have expectations from you, but you from them as well. If you don't like the head honcho's rule, you may choose not to go to that school.

Perhaps there is a good reason for the omission of a guidebook. Maybe the school officials are afraid it would deter people from subbing in their system. After finding out what is expected of you for such a meager salary, some of you may choose not to be a sub at all. If you want to get rich, you'll be better off doing something else. But you know you have to eat and pay the bills like everyone else. So, subbing is a job like any other—that's all I can say about it. If you can stand the kids, you can get by.

Another one of my major gripes is total lack of communication. A classic example of this concerns the bonus, which I previously mentioned which subs were to receive at the end of the year if they put in one hundred days. It was the best-kept secret in the system. I'd heard about the bonus early in the year from a department head, and never heard about it from anyone else again. So, I took the initiative to keep track of the hours I had worked, and made sure I did not turn away too many jobs just in case the rumor was true. (For all I knew it was just a rumor to keep the subs working so there would be no shortage when absenteeism by the faculty was more than the sub system could handle.)

By the end of the year, I received no information concerning the bonus, so I went to see the business manager of the school who you would think would know the answer. Wrong! She laughed at me and said she doubted it was true because money was tight that year. What else is new? Money is always tight when it comes to paying subs. At any rate, she called some mystery woman in charge of subs, who verified that there was a bonus, but the requirement to get it was that a sub work 100 days. That makes a big difference when you consider the fact that subs sometimes work only a half-day.

No sub in the system had ever been formally contacted about bonuses, because subs are not on any mailing list from the schools. That's because money is tight. (I wish money were just as tight for all the companies who insist on sending me a ton of junk mail.)

The position of the substitute implies it is a "temporary" status, which preclude subs from receiving retirement benefits allocated to other school employees. Why can't a sub who puts in an X number of years with the same system be included in benefit programs at a reduced amount, or receive step increases and be eligible for some type of pension plan? I bet if a quality control manager looked over the budget, he/she could probably come up with millions of misappropriated dollars. One of the TV news shows did a segment on this problem in several school systems and came up with some interesting findings. I'm willing to get Ralph Nader involved in our cause as an advocate.

Substitutes are often called upon to do extra "duties." These might include getting children on the buses, which is not terrible unless it requires that you stay longer than the seven hours or so you're getting paid for. Cafeteria duty is much more enjoyable. It entails making sure the children don't throw their peanut butter sandwiches on the ceiling or start food fights. That happens when you're not looking. Some of these kids are very quick and slick. There is also recess duty to contend with as well as various other assignments such as writing a report to leave for the teachers to let them know how the day went. Many of these duties will take the sub beyond the work period she is being paid for—and usually without a thank you from anyone. Gee, the more I write about all these grievances, the happier I become, knowing I don't have to put up with such nonsense anymore. Writing about it is much more fun. It's like a mental enema.

Very often, when a long-term sub cannot be found, a series of subs will be used for class coverage with little or no teaching going on. This is bad for both the subs and the students. I remember a few years back when a math teacher had a medical problem and stayed out much longer than she expected. An influx of subs (most of whom were not math people) came and went daily. For a while, the students were thrilled because they had very little work to do, but eventually, even they got disgusted and began to worry because they were so far behind the rest of the math classes and therefore would not be prepared to take their SAT exams.

When I finally got around to subbing for that teacher (practically every sub in the county had been used) the students began to share their apprehensions with me. My advice to them was to relate this problem to their parents so that the parents could in turn call the administrators to complain. I told that to the head of the math department and he agreed totally. The school launched a nationwide search for a long-term math sub, and ultimately hired one.

Perhaps if subs can relate their concerns to interested parents about the plight of substitutes and the lack of communication and respect given to them, the administration might then sit up and take notice. Parents do have a lot of clout.

I have heard many subs complain about being treated as a nonentity and feeling "invisible." But isn't it amazing how visible they become when a secretary is looking for someone to cover another class or do extra duties? In which case, "invisible" is more desirable.

Emergency coverage has become a growing problem, especially in middle and high schools. A staff member is rarely asked to cover for a colleague if a sub is available. For years it was I who was nearly always the "available sub." I began to feel resentful about giving up one of my free periods. I didn't mind once in a while, but I felt I was being overused. It got to be such a frequent occurrence that I finally confronted the secretaries with "Isn't anyone but Judy ever available?" Evidently they got the message because from then on I was asked to cover much less frequently. The bottom line is that if you let people use you, they will. That's human nature. It took me a long time to learn that lesson, but I finally got it!!

A common concern for new subs is the fear of sending children down to an administrator for disruptive behavior. I don't remember ever being given any instructions on what to do with a disruptive student. But I personally did not need to do it too often, so that when I did, the administrator took the problem seriously.

New subs are afraid that if they send a student out too often, the administrators might think they are incapable of dealing with discipline problems, and might therefore remove them from the substitute list. That was exactly how I felt when I first began subbing. I found, however, that students who gave me problems were themselves marked as disruptive because they gave everyone else problems. Kids know when to toe the line if they know a sub is not just threatening to send them to the office. They will promise and swear to behave. Sometimes they do and sometimes they don't. After giving them one or two chances I would yell, "OUT," and they would leave with their tail between their legs.

So you should trust your judgement on such matters; what I want to warn you about, though, is when you send children to the office, they may not go there but instead hide out in the bathroom.

This is why it is always a good idea to follow-up on their whereabouts. They often return with a lie, such as "Mr. Kindly told me I could come back to the room as long as I say,"I'm sorry." And then they think THAT'S an apology. Sometimes you have to pull out a formal "I'm sorry," from them, and then you know all they're sorry for is that they got reprimanded.

If you think a student may be lying, send him back down to the office to get a note from the secretary stating that the administrator was not in the office. If you don't think you'll be in the building after such an incident, it might be a good idea to leave the teacher a note asking her to follow-up for you. That earns you a lot of credibility with the students so that the next time they see you they know they can't get away with such deceit.

Computer glitches these days are another major gripe. People complain they cannot understand a teacher's name and should spell it out if it's not something as easy as Smith or Jones. Of course, some schools may have more than one teacher with the same last name in which case first and last names should be given along with the subject they teach. Grade level and subjects are often omitted which leaves the sub in the dark, especially at the elementary level. They need to know which bag of tricks to take along with them. In regard to lesson plans, it would be most helpful if the teacher left a message telling where the plans can be found. That would help to eliminate some of the mystery.

Sometimes, a teacher changes her mind about being absent and neglects to inform the sub of the change, but instead just deletes it from the computer. I don't believe there is anything that infuriates a sub more—except possibly the porno flick switcheroo—than to arrive at school to find out the teacher changed her mind and did not take the day off.

There have been many complaints from teachers that there are not always enough subs to go around. The shortage seems to be greater than ever these days. I'm convinced it's because of all of the gripes I've talked about. The system should provide greater incentives for substitutes. And we know what will attract them, don't we? Hint: It's green and has portraits of longhaired men on it. I honestly believe that if the pay were better, the substitute list would be longer which would attract a wider range of people who are better qualified to actually teach a subject without wasting a day doing "busy work." It will also help raise the standards of the system and will eliminate the loss of an instructional day. This has been verified by teachers who use people who can teach their subject matter. Too often, if a teacher is out for a number of days, students will fall behind in their work, in which case the teacher must scramble to teach in one day what was intended to be taught in three. That's not fair to either the students or the teachers.

Because of the lack of substitutes, some teachers have suggested that class coverage by in-staff members be an option and that they be compensated for teaching the extra time. As I mentioned before, there are times when subs need to cover classes other than those they have been assigned and the subs are not given extra compensation. I remember back when more than the normal allotment of snow days had been used, the school day was extended an extra half an hour to make up for the lost time. But subs still received the same pay.

I believe subs could eliminate many workplace disadvantages simply by banding together to present some clout to school boards and politicians at all levels. Every other disadvantaged class in history has done it. Why not subs? We could do a march on Washington, or put on a "Sub Pride" day.

There is now at least one new national organization for subs, the National Substitute Teacher's Alliance, their web site is www. *http://www.nstasubs.org/* Another regional web site is the Substitute Teachers Organization of Palm Beach County, FL, *http:// www.gopbi.com/community/groups/stapbc.*

Epilogue

As I said in the beginning of this book, people begin subbing for various reasons. And for various reasons such as nervous breakdowns or a real job, people leave subbing. In any career, no matter how well you perform your job or how successful you have been, you may ultimately become tapped out.

Because so many of us think we lack the skills to do something else, we continue doing the same thing over and over because it feels comfortable, like Charlie Brown's security blanket, or because we are afraid to explore other avenues. When burnout sets in, it might be too late for a change for some individuals. In my case, the timing was right. I had the need to do something more creative and my two children were finally financially independent. (Actually, that's only a half-truth, because almost everyone I know including myself is in some way assisting his or her children.)

It was also a good time to perform my "Swan Song," since my reviews at school were still positive. (Maybe I should take up ballet now. Nah, I'm too much of a klutz! If I sound confused about a future career, it's simply because I am still trying to decide what I want to be when I grow up.) When I announced that I was going to quit subbing, I got no standing ovation and no farewell parties. What I did get was a few moans and groans from some of the eleventh graders who asked if I could just stay until they graduated. I also heard a few "what will we do without you", comments from some of the teachers. Somehow, I know everyone is surviving without me. However, I must admit, I did like hearing kids say I was their favorite sub and hearing some of the teachers say they would miss me. It gives me a lot of satisfaction knowing I was respected and appreciated. See, you can get respect as a substitute teacher. It just takes hard work and determination to achieve it.

As the years progressed, I discovered a certain flow in my life and I have decided to use those creative skills I was talking about. I am ready to explore new horizons (whatever that means) and try my new wings! However, since my first love is working with children, I have taken a part-time position as a mentor for gifted and talented students who have learning disabilities. It is a rewarding job because dealing with children on a one to one basis is challenging and shows results.

I believe in synchronicity instead of coincidences. I believe that when things are meant to happen, they will happen. Someone up there sees to that. So up until the time of my decision to give up subbing, I had never heard any voices singing out praises for subs. Maybe I've heard other voices which said "Judy, write the book," but never voices of praise. As I had progressed more than half way into the book, I learned that a small group of substitutes in this area had formed an organization in order to better the interests of subs because thus far, they have had no fair representation. I received correspondence in the mail indicating that a few changes were recently implemented in regard to bonuses, savings plans and other considerations being granted to subs. I immediately contacted one of the reps in the group in order to get involved. Although I do not plan to sub anymore, my allegiance and sympathies still lie with my fellow substitutes, because I know they will need a strong support system and advocates who are willing to fight for their rights.

I attended the next meeting, and when the twelve women (male subs apparently have no frustrations or are in denial) introduced themselves, I did likewise, and told them that although I was not planning to sub anymore, I was writing a book on their behalf. I got very favorable responses. What most interested me was that everyone there reaffirmed all the things I had described and discussed in this book. It was as if my words were their voices. (I told you I was hearing voices.) It was almost like a group therapy session. You go to one believing you are the only person with a problem and EUREKA, you find that everyone else feels as rotten as you, only, you never knew it. At least that's the way it's portrayed in the movies.

While I was in my last year of subbing, I asked some subs who had worked with me to share their feelings about their job. I got very little feedback. Occasionally, we would all vent our frustrations about one or two things that went on in the school, but nothing of substance was ever discussed until I attended the aforementioned meeting. This group included a couple of women who had just gotten out of college and some who had subbed as long as seventeen years. Their frustrations were identical.

My plan to get involved in this group was twofold. (I usually hate organizations.) First of all I feel strongly about its cause and want to work as an advocate so substitutes can get as much support as possible. And second, because I knew it would give me the fuel I need to make this a better book. If subs get no support from their system and no training or handbook in order for uniformity to exist, the quality of education becomes undermined for the students.

I hope I have achieved my goal in entertaining, informing and amusing you all with the trials and tribulations of the life of a substitute teacher. And too, I hope I have made people aware of the fact that not only are we professionals, but that we expect to be treated with the same dignity rendered to all other professionals.

On my desk sits a little astrology calendar specifically written for my sign. It is slightly better than the columns you read in the newspaper. In fact, the day I began this book I glanced at the prophetic advice it imparted, and I noticed that it said, "Zero in on educational goals. You won't reach the Promised Land through daydreams. Create a step-by-step plan to achieve ambitions. Be the hero of your own life story." I began writing this book first before I looked at the calendar. It must have been an omen. Get ready, world, here I come!

The author, Judy Mehr, is an accomplished pianist, and is now embarking on a new career as an Energy Healer.)